Men and Women of the Word

MEN AND WOMEN OF THE WORD

45 MEDITATIONS ON BIBLICAL HEROES OF THE FAITH

JAROSLAV VAJDA

CPH™
SAINT LOUIS

Copyright © 1964, 1996 Concordia Publishing House
3558 S. Jefferson Avenue, St. Louis, MO 63118-3968
Manufactured in the United States of America

Library of Congress Cataloging-in Publication Data

Vajda, Jaroslav J:, 1919–
    Men and women of the word : 45 Meditations on biblical heroes of the faith / Jaroslav Vajda.
        p.   cm.
    Reprint (with revisions) of the 1964 edition under the title: follow the king.
    ISBN 0-570-04848-6
    1. Bible—Biography—Meditations. 2. Bible—Meditations.
    I. Title. II. Series.
    BS571.V28   1995
    8'220.9'2—dc20   95-8008

1 2 3 4 5 6 7 8 9 10   04 03 02 01 00 99 98 97 96 95

To my parents,
my first heroes of faith

"Therefore, since we are surrounded by such a
great cloud of witnesses, let us throw off
everything that hinders and the sin that so easily
entangles, and let us run with perseverance the
race marked out for us. Let us fix our eyes on
Jesus, the author and perfecter of our faith."

Hebrews 12:1–2a NIV

CONTENTS

INTRODUCTION   13

ABEL
The Kind of Sacrifice God Accepts   15

ENOCH
Past Death into Life   18

NOAH
A Boat on Dry Land   21

JOB
Not Every Man Has His Price   24

ABRAHAM—I
Letting God Chart the Course   27

ABRAHAM—II
The Ultimate Test   30

SARAH
Too Happy for Words   33

ISAAC
"The Fear of Isaac"   36

JACOB
The Limping Hero   39

JOSEPH
Even in Secret Places   42

MOSES
"By Faith Moses ..."   45

CALEB
The Minority Report   48

JOSHUA
"The Walls Come Tumblin' Down"   51

GIDEON
Add Up a Nobody and God   55

SAMUEL
More than a Hearer   57

DAVID—I
That Mighty Majority of One   60

DAVID—II
Big Man—Big Influence   63

JOSIAH
Like Father ... Unlike Son   66

JONAH
The Reluctant Prophet   69

ELIJAH
At the Bottom of the Barrel   72

ELISHA
Believing Is Seeing   75

NAAMAN'S WIFE'S MAID
A Small and Nameless Witness   78

THE THREE HEBREW CAPTIVES
Try to Stop Us from Worshiping!   81

NEHEMIAH
Cleaning Up Someone Else's Mess   84

MARY
A Vessel Offered to God   87

SIMEON
Standing at the End of the Line   90

THE WISE MEN
Wise Men in Search of a King   93

JOHN THE BAPTIST
None Greater   96

THE TENTH LEPER
In Sickness and in Health   99

THE CENTURION
Table Space for a Foreign Soldier   102

THE MAN BORN BLIND
The Unshakable Witness   105

THE SINFUL WOMAN
No More Imitation Love   108

THE WIDOW OF THE MITES
More than an Offering   111

SYROPHOENICIAN WOMAN
A Treasure Not to Be Lost   114

JOHN
Thunder and Love   117

ZACCHAEUS
A Crook Goes Straight   120

BARTIMAEUS
"...The Blind See ..."   123

THE PENITENT MALEFACTOR
Just, Just in Time   126

PETER
The Fallen Can Stand Too   130

STEPHEN
Killed in Action   133

PAUL
"I Know!"   136

AQUILA AND PRISCILLA
No Longer Two but One   139

TIMOTHY
Beating the Handicap of Birth   142

DORCAS (TABITHA)
"Now There Abideth ... Charity"   145

LYDIA
The Best Purple Anywhere   148

Christ Goes Before

Jaroslav J. Vajda (1987)

RIVERSIDE
Irregular
Carl F. Schalk (1987)

Refrain

Christ goes be - fore, and we are called to fol - low, and all who
fol - low find the Way, the Truth, the Life.

Verses

1 Where is that Way we near de-spaired of find - ing: the way that
2 Where is that Truth we near de-spaired of know - ing: the Truth that
3 Where is that Life we near de-spaired of hav - ing: the Life that

comes from God and leads to God, the realm where God is love and love is
comes from God and leads to God, the pow'r to set us free, the pow'r to
comes from God and leads to God, the hope of glo - ry on - ly Christ can

King, a whole new or - der for a world a - stray?
change, that fac - es Pi - late and the cross and wins?
give, that shat - ters death and grief with Eas - ter joy?

Who wants to live where there's no love like this? Is this the
Who wants to live where there's no peace like this? Is this the
Who wants to live where there's no joy like this? Is this the

To Refrain

King - dom we are read - y for and des - per - ate to find?
Pow - er we are read - y for and des - per - ate to know?
Glo - ry we are read - y for and des - per - ate to have?

INTRODUCTION

FAITH, like love, is "a many-splendored thing." It cannot be described in one word or with just one picture. One has to look at it from many sides to get a glimpse of its glory.

Still, faith is just one thing. It is the sinner taking hold of the life and death of God's Son and holding on for *all* of one's help and life. This every child of God possesses. How large faith is does not matter for salvation. It is either there or it isn't. Where it exists, there is forgiveness received, and the door of heaven is open.

In some people of God the grasp of the new life in Christ is stronger than in others. This does not mean that they are more saved than the weak believers. It does mean that the new life that follows faith does more for God and their fellowmen, and it does more for their life here on earth.

Faith, though unseen except to the eyes of God, shows itself by various virtues. Extraordinary trust in God, patience, courage, love, loyalty, purity, and long-suffering are some of the gifts of grace available to believers. Not all these virtues are present in the same quantity in all believers. In some, one or more of these virtues are outstanding. These are the heroes of faith.

In these pages we shall observe and frankly admire how faith responds to the grace of God. The vessels are all made of clay, even as you and I, but the power poured into them continues to amaze us. Let this "cloud of witnesses" testify to us how strong faith can be and what God can do with the believer.

ABEL

*By faith Abel offered unto God a more excellent
sacrifice than Cain.*
Heb. 11:4

THE KIND OF SACRIFICE GOD ACCEPTS

Not for a long time did God spell out for His crea-
tures the sacrifices they owed Him. And yet Cain and
Abel, the first two brothers, brought sacrifices to the
Lord. It was something they felt they should do because
God was God and they were His creatures.

Each brother took a portion of the product of his
occupation: Cain, a vegetable offering from his farm-
land; Abel, an animal sacrifice from his flocks. The kind
of offering each decided to bring made no difference to
God. Both kinds were later prescribed by God for His
people.

But with Cain and Abel, one offering was acceptable to God, the other was not. This is what led the first
human being born on earth to murder the second. There
was something behind the sacrifices that God saw,
which made one sacrifice acceptable and the other not.

Outwardly they both seemed to be doing the same
thing. What could be more wholesome, decent, or desir-
able than for people to join in a religious service? What

better omen was there for the human race than this voluntary, unforced worship? And yet the sacrifice ended in the first murder in history. There must have been some deep division between the brothers that crippled even their act of worship and prevented them from living together in peace and harmony. God puts His finger on the trouble when He says: "By faith Abel offered unto God a more excellent sacrifice than Cain."

Abel may not have known it, but he was running a risk by being faithful. He was inviting the hostility of his unbelieving brother. There, in the first human family, the division of the human race begins. Jesus exposed it when He said to His small band of followers: "If you were of the world, the world would love its own; but because you are not of the world, but I chose you out of the world, therefore the world hates you" (John 15:19 RSV). John reminded the early Christians of what Abel-like faith provokes when he wrote: "We should love one another, and not be like Cain who was of the evil one and murdered his brother. And why did he murder him? Because his own deeds were evil and his brother's righteous. Do not wonder, brethren, that the world hates you" (1 John 3:11–13 RSV).

Abel might have been safe had he abandoned faith as his brother had and just gone through the motions of worship. If Abel's life had not shone with faith, Cain's evil deeds would not have been shown up, and Cain would not have killed his brother—at least not for that reason. Cain resented the sermon Abel was preaching by merely living. He had to silence that testimony of faith. He thought killing would do it. It didn't stop the voice of Abel's faith. Abel's innocent blood cried to God for vengeance, and his voice goes on speaking to succeeding generations. "He died, but through his faith he is still speaking" (Heb. 11:4 RSV).

What is Abel saying? That it's no use sacrificing to God unless you do it from faith. That God accepts only those sacrifices that come from a broken spirit and a contrite heart. That living or sacrificing without God's approval is futile. That faith divides the human race into two hostile camps. That faith will risk danger and even death to be found among the sheep at the right hand of Christ, to whom the King says: "Come, O blessed of My Father, inherit the kingdom prepared for you from the foundation of the world" (Matt. 25:34 RSV).

By faith Abel was the first to stand in that happy company.

Enoch

By faith Enoch was taken up so that he should not see death; and he was not found, because God had taken him.

Heb. 11:5 RSV

Past Death into Life

ENOCH needs no obituary. He was one of the two persons in all of history who were spared the experience of dying. The other was Elijah.

Not many facts about Enoch's life are available. We do know that he was seven generations removed from Adam. And yet, here was a man who enjoyed some of that intimate relationship that Adam and Eve experienced in the Garden of Eden. Because God was with him, a little piece of Paradise moved about with Enoch as he walked the alien earth.

He was the father of Methuselah, the oldest man in history, who lived to the age of 969 years. Though Enoch's life on earth just equaled the number of days in a year (365), it was probably filled with much more than Methuselah's record number. We are told that "Enoch walked with God" (Gen. 5:24).

Like all the other progenitors of the human race, Enoch was the head of a family, yet he lived in closer communion with God than many a secluded monk or lifelong hermit.

According to Jude, Enoch was also a preacher of righteousness, who reminded his contemporaries that the Lord is coming with legions of angels to judge all men (Jude 14–15). Enoch knew that human beings were created for a blissful eternity with God. He also knew that nothing was more dreadful than to be separated from the heavenly Father.

Furthermore, "before he was taken up he was attested as having pleased God. And without faith it is impossible to please Him" (Heb. 11:5–6 RSV). This sums up the life of Enoch, this and the fact that "he walked with God."

The mark of Enoch's faith was his walking with God. Enoch must have known something of that pure joy and fulfillment that belongs to those who are with God. He must have had a strong foretaste of heaven, which Paul describes as being "forever with the Lord."

One day Enoch was gone. A search was made for him. But there was not a trace of him to be found. "And he was not; for God took him" (Gen. 5:24). Though he was a sinner and the child of a sinner and an heir of death like the rest of us, something intervened to spare Enoch the experience of temporal death. Actually, it was Someone who intervened. It was the One who brought life and immortality to light, the One who killed death when He left it beaten in the grave. Faith in that Someone saved Enoch from dying.

By faith in Him whom Enoch knew in promise as the "Seed of the woman" and whom we know as the Son of God, Enoch bypassed death and went directly into heaven. He who at the grave of Lazarus revealed the opening in the veil of death when He said: "Whoever lives and believes in Me shall never die" (John 11:26 RSV), was with the Father when Enoch was ushered past the last great enemy into unimpaired life with God.

Remember Enoch as the first in that multitude who "walk with God" because they abide in Christ and Christ in them and are just a step away from walking blissfully and completely with the Lord.

NOAH

By faith Noah, being warned by God concerning events as yet unseen, took heed and constructed an ark for the saving of his household; by this he condemned the world and became an heir of the righteousness which comes by faith.

Heb. 11:7 RSV

A BOAT ON DRY LAND

THERE was old Noah, building a boat on dry land, miles from any water that could possibly float it—if it would float at all.

His neighbors watched him and shook their heads. They had wondered about him before, with his different way of living, his criticism of their ways, his worship of God. But now they were sure he was unbalanced. Of all the crazy projects!

And the reason he gave for building the monstrous boat seemed even more preposterous. God, he said, told him that the human race would be destroyed for its wickedness. And this destruction was to happen by a flood. But no one began building an ark except Noah.

This man believed that God was really going to destroy mankind. If the warning was true, the danger was still more than a hundred years away. Yet Noah did not wait to see the rain falling before he gathered tools and materials for the construction of the ark. Whether the rest of the world cared or not, Noah wanted to be ready for the rains when they came.

By pursuing this "crazy" project, Noah was preaching a sermon to the rest of the world. Everyone else, except Noah's family, went on as though nothing would change. They saw no reason for leaving their established way of living. Each day seemed to them like the one just past. And there was no water in sight to float anything the size of Noah's boat. By their behavior they indicated that living in unfaith is nothing to be concerned about, that the warnings of punishment for sin are not to be taken seriously. And so they did nothing about the warning.

When God announced the flood to Noah, Noah was not just to drop his head into his hands and bewail the sad plight of the world. He was to get busy investing time, work, and money into building for tomorrow's rescue, like a man building a fallout shelter long before a possible nuclear attack. By expending the effort it takes to build a shelter, a man says something about his faith or his fears.

Every morning when Noah got up, there stood the ark in his backyard reminding him of God's promise and his neighbors of God's warning. The news of such an unusual project would certainly get around. It would attract the attention of the world just as Christians do when they conscientiously prepare for the Day of Judgment. They plan and act according to their confession in the Creed: "I believe that Jesus Christ will come again to judge the quick and the dead." And they advertise to the world that "ark" by which they expect to be saved.

It wasn't easy for Noah to be such a small minority in the world. All the visible evidence seemed to be on the side of those who mocked the warnings and the provision God had made for rescue. All Noah had to depend on was God's word. And that is where Noah's faith rested.

And the rains came, and the waters rose, and the ark floated, and only Noah and his family were saved!

Exactly as God had said!

JOB

Though He slay me, yet will I trust Him.
Job 13:15

NOT EVERY MAN HAS HIS PRICE

HOW far must a man be pushed before he will let go of God?

Many a person has abandoned faith in God for a comparatively small price. Moses was gone from his people on Mount Sinai for a little over a month, and they turned their backs on the God who had recently liberated them, preferring the worship of Egyptian idols. To please his pagan wives, Solomon, who once walked with God and erected a magnificent temple to His glory, deserted the familiar paths of faith. Demas, Paul's partner in God's plan for winning the world, forsook the company of God's family for the love of the world. For whatever reason people leave God, the price of their treason is usually quite cheap.

It was different with Job. When Satan took on Job to prove to God what he thought was faith's breaking point, he bit into a harder nut than he imagined.

In this unique test of faith, God permitted Satan to deprive Job of 7,000 sheep, 3,000 camels, 500 yoke of oxen, 500 asses, and numerous servants. It had taken Job

24

many years of diligent work to accumulate such wealth. More crippling to Job, however, were the losses he suffered in his own family, his seven sons and three daughters. Yet even these disasters were not heavy enough to press Job into cursing God. As each piece of earthly ballast was pulled away from Job, he soared higher and closer to God. At this point his outlook was: "The LORD gave, and the LORD has taken away; blessed be the name of the LORD" (Job 1:21).

Job had lost all but his wife and his friends, but he still had not been touched in his body. Here, Satan thought, Job's price would be found.

"And Satan answered the LORD and said, Skin for skin! Yes, all that a man has he will give for his life. But stretch out Your hand now, and touch his bone and his flesh, and he will curse You to Your face" (Job 2:4–5 NKJV).

But Satan had underestimated his quarry again. Not even the twisting tortures of a pain-consumed body could pull Job away from God. Neither the disappointment of a despairing wife nor the misunderstanding and unfair accusations of his remaining friends could jar this man loose from his God. With nothing left but a trickle of life, Job would only cry: "Though He slay me, yet will I trust Him" (Job 13:15).

What kind of glue holds a man to God like that? Paul, suffering similar slings of Satan, sang the song of Job thus:

"Who shall separate us from the love of Christ? Shall tribulation, or distress, or persecution, or famine, or nakedness, or peril, or sword? As it is written,

" 'For Thy sake we are being killed all the day long;
we are regarded as sheep to be slaughtered.'

"No, in all these things we are more than conquerors through Him who loved us. For I am sure that neither death, nor life, nor angels, nor principalities, nor things present, nor things to come, nor powers, nor height, nor depth, nor anything else in all creation, will be able to separate us from the love of God in Christ Jesus our Lord" (Rom. 8:35–39 RSV).

By the grace of God, not every man has his price.

ABRAHAM—I

By faith Abraham obeyed when he was called to go out to a place which he was to receive as an inheritance; and he went out, not knowing where he was to go.

Heb. 11:8 RSV

LETTING GOD CHART THE COURSE

LIFE had been pretty good to Abram and his wife, Sarai, back in Ur of the Chaldeans. They were settled comfortably in the fertile Mesopotamian valley. Abram had accumulated a considerable amount of wealth in cattle, silver, gold, servants, and other possessions. By the time he was 75 years old, Abram might have imagined that the struggles were behind him, that he could now relax and enjoy the fruits of many years' labors. Having no children, he and his wife would have only themselves to care for in their retirement.

God, however, had other plans for this man. Abram was meant to enjoy a different kind of inheritance, an altogether different future from that which he had planned for himself. God had chosen Abram to be the first Hebrew, to become the father of a great nation and numerous descendants, and to be the father of believers. Part of this plan involved moving Abram from Babylonia hundreds of miles west to the land of Canaan.

This order of the Lord was one to make anyone hesitate and wonder, especially someone as advanced in years as was Abram. Elderly people do not adjust to new ideas readily. They are reluctant to forsake established patterns and familiar places. Yet this is what God was telling Abram and his wife to do. "Go from your country and your kindred and your father's house to the land that I will show you" (Gen. 12:1 RSV).

Abram was to leave something that was in his hands in favor of something invisible and far away. How could he know it would be better for him in that strange land than it was in his home now? He had taken many a gamble in his life. What reason was there for him to take this one? How could things improve over what he had already? There was, in fact, a good chance that he might lose everything he had gained. He might well become the laughingstock of his friends ("There's no fool like an old fool," they might say), and as for that promise of his becoming a great nation—well, that was even too fantastic to consider!

Though we would expect the average person in Abram's position to say, "No, thank you," the response of Abram sets him apart for all of history and entitles him to special mention in Hebrews 11. In Genesis 12 it is reported: "So Abram went, as the LORD had told him. … Abram was seventy-five years old when he departed from Haran … and they set forth to go to the land of Canaan" (Gen. 12:4–5).

The writer of Hebrews comments that it was "by faith Abraham *obeyed* when he was called to go out to a place which he was to receive as an inheritance; and he went out, not knowing where he was to go" (Heb. 11:8 RSV). Abram traded a permanent residence in Haran for a life of tenting, confident that his Navigator knew where He was leading him. "For he looked forward to the city which has foundations, whose builder and maker is God" (Heb. 11:10 RSV).

So it was that Abram came from the East to the promised land in the West, taking the path of the sun, carrying with him the light of God's grace and becoming a light and life-giving blessing to many future pilgrims by means of the Savior whose day he rejoiced to see.

Abraham—II

*By faith Abraham, when he was tested, offered up
Isaac, and he who had received the promises was
ready to offer up his only son, of whom it was said,
"Through Isaac shall your descendants be named."
He considered that God was able to raise men even
from the dead; hence, figuratively speaking, he did
receive him back.*

Heb. 11:17–19 RSV

The Ultimate Test

WHEN does a believer stop being tested?

Unquestioningly Abram had accepted the challenge of God to forsake Haran and his home and kindred and travel to far-off Canaan. Charting his course and future only by the word of the Lord, he went.

But God was promising Abram more than just the deed to a country of his own, though that was a large enough gift. "l will make of you a great nation," God tells 75-year-old Abram. This meant that sometime thereafter Abram and Sarai would have to have a son. It was fantastic enough to imagine that Sarai, childless up to this time, would have a child, and even more miraculous that the one child would be a male.

After this promise was made to Abram, it lay dormant for 25 years. In the meantime, Sarai, impatient with waiting, urged Abram to have a child by her Egyptian maid Hagar, assuming that the child, Ishmael, would serve as the fulfillment of the promise. But this was not the child of promise. This was a child of the flesh, born of the will of man. The promised son was to be a child of both Abram and Sarai. When 90-year-old Sarai heard this, she laughed. But the Lord rebuked her unbelief, saying: "Is any thing too hard for the LORD?" (Gen. 18:14).

And then the child was born. To Sarai and to Abram. And it was a boy. And the names of Abram ("Exalted Father") and Sarai were changed to Abraham ("Father of a Multitude") and to Sarah. They had entered the age of fulfilled promise.

But not altogether. Now the question arose: Would this child live, and would he have children?

First, would he live? To make this question even more impossible to answer, God confronted Abraham with still another test of faith. He commanded Abraham to take teenaged Isaac up to a mountain and sacrifice him to the Lord. This was the ultimate test. If Isaac should die, then there would be no nation, the carrier of the promise would be eliminated, and Abraham's journey to Canaan would have been pointless.

What would Abraham do with this challenge, not only to his faith in God's promise but to his own fatherly feelings of love for his child?

He obeyed the Lord without question. No one but God the Father can know what feelings went through the heart of Abraham as he prepared to sacrifice his only-begotten Son. Abraham went ahead with the plans with heavy heart, yet knowing that God would somehow carry out His promise, even if He had to resurrect the slain son. Abraham obeyed, "accounting that God was able to raise him up, even from the dead" (Heb. 11:19).

We know the results of the test. God intervened when He saw the trust of Abraham. When the test was over, God announced to Abraham: "By Myself I have sworn ... because you have not withheld your son, your only son, I will indeed bless you, ... because you have obeyed My voice" (Gen. 22:16–18 RSV).

Nothing about Abraham was as important to the Lord as his great and enduring faith. Not his wealth or his prestige. But "[Abraham] believed the Lord; and He reckoned it to him as righteousness" (Gen. 15:6 RSV). Abraham passed all the tests, including the ultimate one, that of loving the Lord more than his own son.

Willing to suffer every loss, Abraham gained God, and with God, everything.

SARAH

God has made laughter for me; every one who hears will laugh over me.

Gen. 21:6 RSV

TOO HAPPY FOR WORDS

IF God weren't soberly serious when He makes His fantastic promises, many of them would sound quite ridiculous. That He should sacrifice His only Son for selfish and obstinate rebels sounds so absurd as to be almost funny. What human being in his right mind would do such a thing? Isn't it sensible to give no more than you get? To throw away your life or that of your beloved for someone who doesn't deserve it and may very well completely forget or ignore your sacrifice—sounds a little silly. Some people laugh when they hear this.

Sarah had to laugh and her husband guffawed when God announced to Abraham in all earnestness: "As for Sarai your wife, you shall not call her name Sarai, but Sarah shall be her name. I will bless her, and moreover I will give you a son by her; I will bless her, and she shall be a mother of nations; kings of peoples shall come from her. Then Abraham fell on his face and laughed, and said to himself, 'Shall a child be born to a man who is a hundred years old? Shall Sarah, who is ninety years old, bear a child?' " (Gen. 17:15–17 RSV). They laughed—not because God's promise was funny, but because His methods seemed so ridiculous.

God heard the laughter and remembered it in the name of the promised child, Isaac. "God said, 'No, but Sarah your wife shall bear you a son, and you shall call his name Isaac' " [*meaning, He laughs*] (Gen. 17:19 RSV). Whenever they would call out to their son, they would recall their laughter of unbelief which God changed to laughter of joy fulfilled.

As surely as time rolls on, the child was conceived and born. "And Sarah said: 'God has made laughter for me; every one who hears will laugh over me' (Gen. 21:6 RSV). It was no dream that she had had. This was no unreal symbol of joy that God had promised Sarah and Abraham. This was a flesh-and-blood, bawling, waving, kicking baby boy. Sarah could hold him and nurse him and love him as the delight of her life. Now she could lift up her head before her insolent servant Hagar. She would no longer have to listen to the humiliating taunts of that woman and her son. She had a son of her own, and her husband had an heir—and the Messiah had an ancestor! It was enough to make her laugh. Isaac (he laughs): What a grand joke God played on doubt and sadness, on shame and disgrace! Come on, everybody, laugh! "God has made me laugh, so that all who hear will laugh with me" (NKJV).

Isaac was given to make Sarah's joy complete. Another only Child of His Father, born in a miraculous manner, made His mother sing with joy: "My soul magnifies the Lord, and my spirit has rejoiced in God my

Savior!" This Child, given also to *us*, born to *us*, turns our mourning to tearful laughter as we sing: "When the LORD brought back the captivity of Zion, we were like those who dream. Then our mouth was filled with laughter, and our tongue with singing. Then they said among the nations, 'The LORD has done great things for them. The LORD has done great things for us, whereof we are glad. ... Those who sow in tears shall reap in joy" (Ps. 126:1–3, 5 NKJV).

We have an idea of what Sarah's joy was like. We sense it as we ponder how such a wonder could happen and why it should happen, of all people, to us! It makes us almost too happy for words. About all we can do is laugh with tears streaming down our face.

ISAAC

And Isaac said to his father Abraham, "My father!" And he said, "Here am I, my son."

Gen. 22:7 RSV

"THE FEAR OF ISAAC"

WHEN do you stop being a child? By the laws of the state, at the age of 18 or 21. In your relationship to God, never.

We are always and forever the children of God. When we know this, we know how it really is between us and God. As long as we live we are to pray: "Our Father." And when we breathe our last, the best prayer our lips can utter is that of the 33-year-old Son of God: "Father, into Your hands I commend My spirit."

We are out of step with reality when we step out of this Father-child relationship with God. This special relationship is one of complete devotion to the Father, an eagerness to do the will of the Father, and a profound reluctance to displease the Father. No one lived this relationship more perfectly than Jesus.

Isaac was like our Lord in so many filial ways. He was a child by a special promise. He was an only son, greatly loved by his father. He was named by God and circumcised on the eighth day.

As a young man (Josephus estimated Isaac to have been 25 years old), Isaac was led under orders of God by his father to be sacrificed on a mountain. Isaac did not rebel at the maneuverings of his father in that direction. He even carried the wood for his sacrifice up the mountainside and permitted himself to be laid on the altar. There was no doubt in his father's mind that since this was the will of God, God could and would raise his son from the dead, if necessary, to fulfill His promise of the Messiah.

Isaac lived out his life in a Christlike pattern of submissiveness to the Lord's will. He believed that it is God who lays out the plan for our life and that it is up to us to conform to that plan so that God may accomplish His purposes. He showed his respect for God's wisdom by doing the will of God as God wanted it to be done.

Isaac's son Jacob used to recall this special quality of his father and referred to it as the "fear of Isaac." It was the same quality that was so prominent in Isaac's Seed, Jesus, toward His heavenly Father, whom He was determined to obey in the form of a servant even to the death of the cross.

God Himself enjoys such a childlike stance toward Him. He delights in identifying Himself as "the God of Abraham, *Isaac*, and Jacob."

The child is also blessed when he stands in such a relationship toward God. To Isaac's confidential call, "My father," his father, Abraham, lovingly responded, "Here am I, my son." When God's children cry, "Abba, Father," "as a father pities his children, so the LORD pities those who fear Him" (Ps. 103:13 NKJV).

There is no warmth or closeness to compare with the love between the heavenly Father and His children. Isaac knew it long before he got to meet the perfect Child of God whose preview he was privileged to be. He preferred never to grow out of God's family.

JACOB

I will not let You go, unless You bless me.
Gen. 32:26b RSV

THE LIMPING HERO

THERE, hard to understand, is the name of Jacob in the 11th chapter of Hebrews. We can readily see why Abraham and Moses are in that select list of heroes—but Jacob? We wonder.

And so we examine the life of the man after whom the Israelites were named to see what was so heroic about it. And what we discover is a limping hero.

Prior to his birth, God had informed his mother that Jacob would rule over his firstborn twin brother, Esau. Rebekah favored Jacob and prompted him to deceive his father Isaac to get the birthright. Jacob had already bought the birthright from his brother for a pottage of lentils. With and without encouragement, Jacob obtained the advantages he wanted honestly or by craft. When he set his heart on something, he permitted nothing to stand in his way. He would sacrifice or cheat, work or wrestle for what he wanted.

It took him 14 years of hard labor to get the wife he wanted. He had to struggle against the treachery of his uncle Laban and suffer the kind of deceit he himself had practiced. Finally he broke away to go to his homeland, a rich and prosperous man. He had wanted much and he had obtained much. Most other men would have been satisfied long before they achieved what Jacob had.

But not Jacob. All that he had received in the way of material possessions would fall out of his hands one day. All this he would leave behind. There was one blessing, however, that he simply had to have above all others.

And then, one day, on his return to Canaan, Jacob was left standing all alone. He had sent his family on ahead to be safe in case Esau would be unforgiving and would kill him. That night Jacob wrestled with an unknown adversary until the break of day. As in every other effort, Jacob was determined to win. He would not let go of the man even when the man threw Jacob's thigh out of joint.

"I will not let You go," said Jacob, "unless You bless me." At this the man asked Jacob: "What is your name?" And he answered: "Jacob." Then the stranger said: "Your name shall no more be called Jacob, but Israel [He who strives with God], for you have striven with God and with men, and have prevailed." And there He blessed Jacob. "So Jacob called the name of the place Peniel [The face of God], saying, 'For I have seen God face to face, and yet my life is preserved.' The sun rose upon him as he passed Peniel, limping because of his thigh" (Gen. 32:28–32 RSV).

Jacob must have wanted very badly what only God could give him. That coveted blessing meant more to him than all he could gain by his own efforts and scheming. It was like a Holy Grail before him, in his dreams and in his heart. No one can approve of the weaknesses and methods of Jacob in getting what he wanted. But he can be envied for his consuming obsession with the gracious blessing of God.

Some gifts have to be wrestled and prayed out of the hand of God. There is some of the heroism of Jacob in every believer who will not leave a visit in God's house or stand up from his prayers unless he can depart with the Lord's blessing.

As we watch Jacob limping off into the sunrise, we see how badly someone can want what only God can give.

JOSEPH

How then can I do this great wickedness, and sin against God?

Gen. 39:9 RSV

EVEN IN SECRET PLACES

SOFTLY the door to the lavish Egyptian chambers closed. Soon there was no sound in the room but the purring of an attractive woman's voice. Potiphar was out of town, and his wife was about to arrange herself an affair with a handsome servant of the household.

Young Joseph, the servant, was far from home. He was completely on his own, far from the watchful eye of a father who idolized him, and brothers who would gloat over any slip he might make. Now, behind closed doors, who would know what Joseph thought—or said—or did? The setting was ready-made for a modern novel or motion picture.

To the surprise of Potiphar's wife and that of the jaded reader of contemporary fiction, Joseph backed away from the temptation. Could it be that he wasn't virile? Wasn't this the fulfillment of any red-blooded young man's fantasy? He was right in the heart of the wild-oats-sowing age. Was he perhaps unsure of himself? Was he afraid of what his master would do if he learned of his wife's escapade? Or would he later regret passing up such a rare opportunity for tasting forbidden pleasures?

It was none of this. Joseph was a very positive young man, well prepared for such an unexpected situation. Years later he would help the entire Egyptian nation to be ready for the hazards of seven lean years by storing up provisions during the seven fat years. Now, alone, Joseph was armed for personal combat against sin because he had accumulated an arsenal in his earlier, sheltered years. He was simply doing what comes naturally to a young man who gets his ideals from God and maintains an intimate relationship with God. Had Potiphar's wife known this, she would not have been astounded to hear him say: "How can I do this great wickedness, and sin against God?"

She did not expect an answer like that. But God did. God loved this young man, and the young man reacted to God's grace by seeking to please God in every way. "How can a young man cleanse his way? By taking heed according to Your Word" (Ps. 119:9 NKJV). Joseph was regulating his way of living by that Word. He was giving God all of himself, body as well as soul.

"With my whole heart have I sought You: Oh, let me not wander from Your commandments. Your Word I have hidden in my heart, that I might not sin against You" (Ps. 119:10–11 NKJV). The pull of God's love was stronger for Joseph than the contrary pull of what Potiphar's wife called "love."

Science has devised a method by which a missile can be directed in its flight by preset controls. It performs its mission without radio directions from a base. The mechanism within the rocket follows its predirected course and heads unerringly for its destination. The secret is the gyroscope, which holds steady to the course regardless of the push and pull of its surrounding parts.

Joseph was held by an inner gyroscope to the path that pleases God. The distraction of a moment's pleasure could not divert him from that course.

The temptation was repeated. This time the sound of Joseph's running feet echoed through the chambers.

And Potiphar's wife stood alone with Joseph's empty garment in her hands.

MOSES

But since then there has not arisen in Israel a prophet like Moses.

Deut. 34:10 NKJV

"BY FAITH MOSES ..."

MOSES was like a well-equipped army lacking only courage to be victorious. The raw materials that went to make up the man were impressive. He grew up in the palace of the mighty Egyptian Pharaoh. He was educated in the highest wisdom of one of the most advanced cultures in history. He knew his way around the royal court, the intrigues that had to be played, the pressures that could be applied to get what you wanted. He could evaluate the forces of this world power. And during a 40-year exile, Moses learned the wilderness between Egypt and his countrymen's homeland as well as an Indian scout knew the terrain of primitive America.

Only one ingredient had to be applied to this man's outstanding traits and training to make him useful to God in delivering a nation from foreign bondage: and that was faith. Moses had it.

We see how it worked in him to carry out the daring plan of God.

God used Moses' parents to plant the faith in him. "By faith Moses, when he was born, was hidden three months by his parents, because they saw he was a beautiful child; and they were not afraid of the king's command" (Heb. 11:23 NKJV). This was the first push Moses had in the direction of his destiny. His life would be a constant choosing of the higher alternative, even though each choice would place his life in danger. The first choice of faith was made for Moses by his parents, when they boldly trusted that God would preserve the baby's life against the decree of Pharaoh that all Jewish male children should be killed.

"By faith Moses, when he became of age, refused to be called the son of Pharaoh's daughter; choosing rather to suffer affliction with the people of God than to enjoy the pleasures of sin, esteeming the reproach of Christ greater riches than the treasures in Egypt; for he looked to the reward" (Heb. 11:24–26 NKJV). There came a time when Moses had to choose between the advantage of palace living as an adopted Egyptian or the hazard of identifying himself with his own afflicted people. The allure of the court life was strong; the treasures available to him were stunning. But Moses weighed these advantages against the lot of his people and God's people— and he made the choice of faith, certain that the reward of such a choice would far outweigh what he was giving up personally.

"By faith he forsook Egypt, not fearing the wrath of the king; for he endured as seeing Him who is invisible" (Heb. 11:27 NKJV). The king in Egypt and his armed forces were very visible. The shouts of the taskmasters were heard above the cries of the groaning Hebrew slaves. But Moses saw another force, mightier than Egypt's. He heard another Voice, more compelling than the oppressor's. Following that Voice and trusting in that Force, Moses chose to defend his oppressed countrymen, and went into exile. The last bridge behind him was burned.

He returned, however, by another bridge, by the bridge of God's promise to deliver His people at all costs. "By faith he kept the Passover and the sprinkling of blood, lest he who destroyed the firstborn should touch them" (Heb. 11:28 NKJV). This was the final test of faith for Moses and the Israelites before the doors of their imprisonment would burst open. They had to believe that the smearing of the spotless lamb's blood on their doorposts would preserve them from the visit of the angel of death. And this act of faith, repeated by every child of God who trusts in the blood of God's Lamb on Calvary's cross, was initiated by Moses before the final plague struck.

"By faith they passed through the Red Sea as by dry land, whereas the Egyptians, attempting to do so, were drowned" (Heb. 11:29 NKJV). Without faith Moses and the Israelites would have drowned as did the Egyptians when they reached the Red Sea in their flight from slavery. But faith opened a path for them through this obstacle that destroyed the faithless.

Faith changed the timid, stammering shepherd into a courageous emancipator. Faith saw the plan of God and carried it out. Faith placed all the native abilities and advantages of a favored man into the hands of God and said: Use them to Your glory.

CALEB

*But My servant Caleb, because he has a different
spirit and has followed Me fully, I will bring into
the land into which he went, and his descendants
shall possess it.*

Num. 14:24 RSV

THE MINORITY REPORT

THE majority isn't always right. Though it carries
the weight of numbers, it can be very blind to the facts.
Caleb knew this and acted accordingly.

The children of Israel had been on the march from
Egypt for a comparatively short time. They had arrived
near the border of the Promised Land. Before proceeding
to their goal, God directed Moses to dispatch 12 spies
into the land to find out the strength of the squatters
occupying His people's inheritance. Each of the spies
was the chief man of his tribe.

The 12 went, disguised, through the land of their
fathers for 40 days. They were amazed at what they saw.
Some of the evidence they were able to bring back: a
cluster of grapes so huge it took two men to carry it. For
the rest of the report the Israelites would have to rely on
the observations of the spies and their considered conclusions.

The 12, however, were not unanimous in their report. They had all seen the same things, but they were of two conflicting opinions.

Ten of the spies stood before the assembled refugees and presented their report. "The land flows with milk and honey, but its inhabitants are dreadfully strong. We seemed like grasshoppers compared with them," they whined. It was a report completely lacking in confidence. Nevertheless it carried with the people. They were ready to accept the fearful conclusions of the 10. The minority report could hardly be heard above the lamentation. "All the congregation raised a loud cry; and the people wept that night. And all the people of Israel murmured against Moses and Aaron. ... And they said to one another, 'Let us choose a captain and go back to Egypt' " (Num. 14:1–2, 4 RSV).

To forestall the revolt, Joshua and Caleb, the two remaining spies, pleaded with the nation to reconsider its decision. "If the LORD delights in us," they said, "He will bring us into this land and give it to us. ... The LORD is with us; do not fear them." They got nowhere. Rather, "all the congregation said to stone them with stones" (Num. 14:8–10 RSV).

The people were ready to abandon their journey on into the land of promise. But Caleb could not see it. They had been brought this far so that they might inherit the land of Canaan. The situation looked entirely different to Caleb than it did to the 10 spies. The longer he compared the forces opposing Israel with the proved might of the Lord, the more they shrank in size and terror.

Caleb's name happens to mean "bold" or "dog." It

couldn't have fit him better. Like a dog he clamped his teeth on his objective, tussled with it and shook it, and would not let go. Doggedly he kept insisting that they would win with the Lord. Let the others go back to Egypt or into the barren wilderness, he was for plunging ahead, counting on the Lord's faithfulness to His people.

The majority did return to the wilderness, but Caleb made it to the Promised Land—some 40 years later. God condemned Israel to wandering in the wilderness outside its homeland's boundaries for the number of years equal to the number of days spent by the spies in Canaan. Of all who had left Egypt above the age of 20, not one would enter the Promised Land except Caleb and that other member of the minority, Joshua.

The majority left their bones in the wilderness and their names in oblivion. The majority wasn't right after all. The truth was on the side of those who looked at the facts through the eyes of faith.

JOSHUA

*By faith the walls of Jericho fell down after they had
been encircled for seven days.*

Heb. 11:30 RSV

"THE WALLS COME TUMBLIN' DOWN"

FOR seven days Joshua and his people walked
around their problem. On the seventh day they walked
around it seven times. This was no desperate pacing
about, looking for a way out of a hopeless situation. This
marching of Israel around Jericho was an act of faith, a
hopeful anticipation of a solution to their problem. On
the seventh day their "problem" collapsed in dust before
them. It is written that their faith caused the walls to fall
down.

Under the leadership of Moses the children of Israel
had been trained for 40 years for this critical hour at the
borders of the Holy Land. Each day of those four
decades they had to depend on the providential care of
God. A wandering nation of two million refugees has a
great many needs. At the beginning of their long journey
God said to them: "Behold, I will rain bread from heaven
for you; and the people shall go out and gather a
day's portion every day" (Ex. 16:4 RSV). And at the end
of the journey He told them: "I have led you forty years

in the wilderness; your clothes have not worn out upon you, and your sandals have not worn off your feet" (Deut. 29:5 RSV).

Over and over again during that time God had delivered them out of the grasp of superior forces. Fierce enemies had been swept before them. And they knew it was not their own prowess but the arm of the Lord which had gotten them the victory.

Even the obstacles of nature had been removed for them in miraculous ways. The Red Sea opened a path for them, water gushed forth in the desert, and poisonous snakes were driven out of their camp. And the Lord's hand was behind it all.

Now they stood at the very boundaries of the land their forefathers had left 470 years earlier. Before them lay the fields and vineyards "flowing with milk and honey." All they had to do was reach out and possess the land.

One final barrier barred the way to the land of promise. Just across the Jordan, which parted for them as did the Red Sea, rose the formidable walls of Jericho. Weapons had not yet been invented which could demolish those defenses. If they were to try to take the city themselves, they would run the risk of depleting a large part of their manpower. They might even be prevented from advancing beyond this point. Only those walls separated them from their goal and dream, freedom and promise. But what walls they were!

God had not brought them this far to desert them now. He would continue to fight their battles for them. He told Joshua, the successor of Moses, that He would remove that final barrier for them. They were to march around the city once each day for seven days, and seven times on the seventh day, and at the sound of the trumpets, to shout.

Joshua had just taken over the leadership of the nation. Now he had to make a decision that would affect his subsequent leadership among the people. He could either follow these "unbelievable" directives of the Lord and let the Lord take the city and the credit for the victory, or he could substitute a plan of his own in which his own military skill would shine and, *if* the city could be taken, make a name for himself.

Without hesitation, Joshua relayed the orders God had given him. They would take the city—with the help of God. Like that other "Joshua" (even the name is the same—Joshua/Jesus) who came centuries later, this Joshua's motto was, "My food is to do the will of Him who sent me, and to accomplish His work" (John 4:34 RSV). Like that greater "Joshua" he would lead God's people into the land of promise by faith in the one who made the promise.

The faith of Joshua inspired the people to similar faith, and "the people shouted, and the trumpets were blown. ... and the wall fell down flat, so that the people went up into the city, every man straight before him, and they took the city" (Joshua 6:20 RSV).

After this the land soon became theirs by possession. Faith had removed the final obstacle, the wall of separation, between them and the land of promise.

Jericho reminds us of the wall around which we pace restlessly and hopelessly unless we follow that latter "Joshua" and watch Him demolish that barrier of transgressions for us. That wall between us and our Promised Land falls flat before faith in Him who has melted it down with His blood. Over those ruins the children of God march victoriously into the Eternal City after their "Joshua," their Savior.

GIDEON

Pray, Lord, how can I deliver Israel? Behold, my clan is the weakest in Manasseh, and I am the least in my family.

Judges 6:15 RSV

ADD UP A NOBODY AND GOD

ELECTRONIC computers can solve in minutes problems that would take individuals days and years to resolve. They work fine with figures and testable variables. But they are unable to compute the influence of one factor which alters situations, defies mathematical and logical predictions, and brings success out of predictable failure. They meet their match with that quantity called faith.

What would a computer suggest in a situation like this? A nation of several million people had been subdued by a hostile invader. The conquered Israelites had to hide out in caves and could not harvest a crop in seven years. Each planting was destroyed by the Midianites and other hostile tribes surrounding their country. In this desperate situation, what would the computer recommend?

Find a leader to lead a revolt? Store up a vast supply of munitions, rise up against the oppressor and defeat him by sheer force of numbers? But the land was without a ready-made leader, anxious to launch a suicide attack against such a formidable enemy. And of 32,000 possible recruits for a counterattack, 22,000 were cowards by their own admission. And of the 10,000 remaining potential troops, 9,700 could not pass a basic test of survival. So the computer has only 300 men to work with. And for a leader … ? Well, God would suggest a furtive farmer by the name of Gideon, a man of many doubts and qualms, a man of towering inferiority, who responds to the suggestion by pleading: "Pray, Lord, how can I deliver Israel? Behold, my clan is the weakest in Manasseh, and I am the least in my family." (Judges 6:15 RSV)

To these potentials, unpromising as they are, add these statements of God: "Do not I send you?" and "I will be with you," and see what happens. The former farmer and his valiant 300 surround the Midianite camp in the night, on a signal they smash empty jars, blow trumpets, wave burning torches, and shout: "A sword for the Lord and for Gideon!"

What would the computer say to that? Zero? A suicidal game?

What does the record say? "And all the army ran; they cried out and fled" (Judges 7:21 RSV).

When the rest of Israel saw the enemy routed, it was an easy matter to run them down and destroy them. Enemy casualties ran more than 120,000 armed men.

The unknown factor must have done it. The unmeasurable element called "faith in the true God" proved all human calculations wrong.

And a man called "Gideon" is inserted into the list of heroes in Hebrews 11.

SAMUEL

Be doers of the word, and not hearers only, deceiving yourselves.

James 1:22 RSV

MORE THAN A HEARER

HEBREWS 11 and James 1 are separated by just a few pages in the Bible. Still there is a close connection between the two, for the heroes of faith listed in Hebrews are men and women who demonstrate the admonition of James: "Be doers of the word, and not hearers only, deceiving yourselves. ... He who looks into the perfect law, the law of liberty, and perseveres, being no hearer that forgets but a doer that acts, he shall be blessed in his doing" (James 1:22, 25 RSV).

The first time we see Samuel, he is a young boy, boarding with the high priest, Eli. When the voice called Samuel's name in the night, Samuel was told to answer: "Speak, Lord, for Your servant hears." From the very beginning of his life, Samuel was a hearer of God's Word. He listened carefully to every word that came to him from the mouth of God. God had listened favorably to the prayer of Samuel's mother for the gift of a son. Now that son spent his life hearing the Word of the Lord.

Hearing itself is no great achievement, though it is

the necessary starting point for a life of service to God. That life is stillborn unless the hearing produces action.

Samuel heard more than the Word of God. In all parts of the land he heard grumbling about conditions. And the people had something to complain about. Many things needed correction. Even their religious leaders, such as Eli, left much to be desired. Privately and publicly, people expressed their dissatisfaction with things as they were. But then, as now, hardly anyone went beyond shaking his head and clucking his tongue. If a man set about to do something about the wrongs in the land, he was an unusual person. Such a person would qualify for a place on a special list of heroes. And that's where we find Samuel.

From God, Samuel had learned what a man and the people of God should be. He saw for himself what had been deformed from the image that God had made. What was needed was a drastic and thorough reformation. Many people were ready to change if only someone would get up and lead them.

To move from passive hearing to active doing is not easy or natural. Most people find it so challenging or unattractive or dangerous or lonely that they content themselves with curbstone coaching. They refuse to take a definite stand for fear of losing their safe position. Or they refrain from expressing a conviction in order to leave themselves free to criticize the people who do. Samuel could have chosen that safe and undisturbed way for himself. Eli was giving him a lesson in letting things drift as they will. There is a promise of security in keeping your neck in while the votes are being taken and waiting to see which way the majority is going.

Samuel could not and would not be satisfied with just listening. When the Lord speaks, He tells His people to *do* something, to act for Him on behalf of sinners. When worshipers rise from listening and proceed to doing, the kingdom of God moves, the body of Christ grows, the grace of God floods the land with blessing, and prodigal children of God see the signposts directing them home.

Only faith can move mountains. Only faith can move a man or a woman from hearing to doing. Samuel had it, and he moved and acted. He reformed the land which had strayed from the Lord.

And the land was cleansed. The people had reason to stop complaining. It had taken some doing. It had taken someone to do the doing. And the Lord found His someone in Samuel.

DAVID—I

I come to you in the name of the LORD of hosts.
1 Sam. 17:45 RSV

THAT MIGHTY MAJORITY OF ONE

BOOMING across the Valley of Elah came the bloodcurdling boasts of Goliath, the Philistine champion. Towering some 10 feet high, armed with heavy mail, and brandishing a spear the size of a weaver's beam, the spectacular giant of Gath roared at the cringing Israelites: "I defy the ranks of Israel this day; give me a man, that we may fight together" (1 Sam. 17:10). No response came from King Saul and his warriors except the sound of shaking knees and fluttering hearts.

The odds were impossible. Nowhere in the forces of Israel was there a man to match the strength and size of Goliath. The giant had many a notch in his lance to remind them of the foolish foes who dared take up his challenges. And yet, unless the Israelites came up with someone to fight the Philistine, they were in danger of losing their independence, their country, and, quite possibly, their lives.

The fact was Goliath had an equal on the other side whom few of the Israelites remembered in this dark hour. They should have remembered. He had won many a victory for them in the past, sometimes single-handed against enemies stronger than the Philistines. But they had forgotten. They felt that now they were on their own. This challenge seemed different. Now they were a nation like others, with armies and a king. Now they expected to fight their own battles alone in the only way nations know: with superior skill and armor. But they simply didn't have it. And that is why they waited for the onslaught paralyzed with fear.

One person in Israel remembered their superior advantage. When he was older, he recorded that advantage in songs to be recited over and over again: "The LORD is the strength of my life; of whom shall I be afraid?" (Ps. 27:1 NKJV). "Be of good courage, and He shall strengthen your heart, all you who hope in the LORD" (Ps. 31:24 NKJV).

Israel was at the point of a drowning man clutching at a straw. If they were going to be beaten anyway, why not give David a chance? Yet even now they weren't ready to go as far as David in their trust in God. They would load him down with the bulky armor in which they had been placing so much of their confidence.

David took off the armor, chose five stones from a brook, grasped his shepherd's staff, and unwound his sling. Then he strode out into that empty valley. Invisibly Someone else walked alongside. David felt Him there. "The LORD is my Shepherd; ... though I walk through the valley of the shadow of death, I will fear no evil: for Thou art with me; Thy rod and Thy staff, they comfort me" (Ps. 23:1, 4). The Lord made him audacious.

Once more the giant laughed at the ridiculous

sight—and then fell dead with a stone embedded in his skull.

Come, little David, play on your harp, and sing hallelujah! It can be done. Any odds can be faced, every foe can be beaten—with the arm of the Lord!

How would David have said it?

" 'If it had not been the LORD who was on our side,' Let Israel now say—'if it had not been the LORD who was on our side, when men rose up against us, then they would have swallowed us up alive, when their wrath was kindled against us; then the waters would have overwhelmed us, the stream would have gone over our soul; then the swollen waters would have gone over our soul.' Blessed be the LORD, who has not given us as prey to their teeth. Our soul has escaped as a bird from the snare of the fowlers; the snare is broken, and we have escaped. Our help is in the name of the LORD, who made heaven and earth" (Ps. 124 NKJV).

DAVID—II

I have found David the son of Jesse, a man after My own heart, who will do all My will.

Acts 13:22 NKJV

BIG MAN—BIG INFLUENCE

IF Lord Acton's dictum is true, that "power tends to corrupt, and absolute power corrupts absolutely," then the man in high places who walks humbly before his God is a rare creature indeed.

Looking over the index of the world's great, we do not find many who have successfully overcome the hazard to worship power or to use it only for their own advantage. Even among the Bible's listing of strong men, only a few are said to be men after the Lord's own heart. Solomon doesn't make the roll call of heroes in Hebrews 11, nor do Nebuchadnezzar or Ahab or Alexander the Great or any of the Roman emperors or any of the Ptolemies of Egypt. But there is David's name.

Give the average man unusual power or prestige, and watch him change his values, puff up with pride, and trample others in his drive for the top. Even very few Christians can stand off the temptations that come with riches and power. Knowing the hazards of wealth, Jesus warned His disciples: "Truly, I say to you, it will be hard for a rich man to enter the kingdom of heaven. Again I tell you, it is easier for a camel to go through the eye of a needle than for a rich man to enter the kingdom of God" (Matt. 19:23–24 RSV).

David successfully overcame this temptation to consider himself the lord of his own life just because he was lord over others. He remembered his early shepherd life, out of which he was chosen by God to be anointed king of Israel. The Lord was his Shepherd; David was always the sheep reposing in the Shepherd's arm.

David remembered also that the Lord was his Deliverer as He was the Deliverer of His people from the hand of the Philistines and Goliath. Though great and mighty enemies fell before his arms, David acknowledged privately and publicly that it was the arm of the Lord that had gotten him the victory.

David remembered that he had not selected himself to be king, nor did he fight his way to the throne of Israel. The kingdom fell into his lap. And all because the Lord had His eye on David and considered David a man after His own heart. The Lord liked the way David submitted himself to God's will, how he delighted in the Lord, how he recognized the grace of God in choosing him, how he loved the Law of the Lord, how he longed for the coming of the Messiah. This man was a model ruler, a man who would use his great influence for the good of many.

Like all saints, David was also a sinner. In wrongdoing he is, of course, not to be imitated. David himself suffered anguish and punishment for it, and regretted it deeply. He was torn apart by remorse and sincerely repented of his transgression, feeling bad not that he had been caught and judged for sinning, but that he had disobeyed and offended his loving Lord. "Against You, You only, have I sinned, and done this evil in Your sight," he wept (Ps. 51:4 NKJV). Many a sleepless night he was troubled by his conscience.

And then he rose from the depths of contrition to say with confidence: "I acknowledged my sin to You, and my iniquity I have not hidden. I said, 'I will confess my transgressions to the LORD,' and You forgave the iniquity of my sin" (Ps. 32:5 NKJV).

What a man! What a believer! What a child of God! No wonder that God delighted to call David His servant! Here was an example to the world of what a ruler could be. God could accomplish His purposes in a man like this. God could use a man like this to preview the glorious kingdom of Christ.

Millions venerate David as a mighty man, a historical hero. His star is displayed proudly by a proud nation. Millions have thanked God for the gift of David, the psalmist and prophet. But the best accolade of all is that of the Lord, who said: "I have found David a man after my own heart."

JOSIAH

In the eighth year of his reign, while he was yet a boy, he began to seek the God of David his father.

2 Chron. 34:3 RSV

LIKE FATHER ... UNLIKE SON

"THE king is dead. Long live the king!" An age-old pattern was repeating itself. The ruler died. His successor was put in his place.

Amon, king of Judah, was dead. In an age of violence it was still shocking to the people to have their king assassinated in his own palace by his own countrymen. But not many in the kingdom were sorrowful to see him gone. The Judeans had had enough of Amon. He had done little or nothing to gain the respect of his subjects. Amon had chosen to follow the example of most of the regents before him. "He did what was evil in the sight of the LORD, as Manasseh his father had done" (2 Chron. 33:22 RSV). His father had sacrificed to images, and Amon did too. He got what he wanted: the kingdom. But he held it for just two fleeting years. By the age of 24 all he had grasped slipped through his death-stiffened fingers. Summing up, Amon's was not the kind of life to attract hero worshipers.

Amon was dead. Soon thereafter, in the traditional ceremony, his little eight-year-old son, Josiah, was placed on the tottering and tarnished throne of Judah. Weighing the law of averages, his subjects could expect little more of Josiah than they had of the kings before him. For many generations it had been "like father like son." With the rare exception of kings like Jotham and Hezekiah, most of the other apples did not fall far from the royal family tree.

Why should Josiah be different? Many must have wondered if he would be, including Josiah himself. Sometime during those eye-opening years between 8 and 16, Josiah must have reflected on his life, past and future. Could he possibly break the evil and selfish pattern set by his father and grandfather? Or was he chained by the forces of heredity and environment to be the same kind of person? Oh, the dreams were there, fresh, bright, and beckoning, but would they come true? Can a child reverse the pattern of his parents? Would Josiah be different from all other teenage dreamers who visualize a dazzlingly different life but catch themselves slipping into the same garments of mediocrity or frustration their parents have discarded?

Josiah had one bit of influence working for his benefit. His mother was not like his father. He could plant his feet in her footprints. They might take him away from his father's pattern.

Josiah found more than human encouragement and resources. With youthful zeal and determination he began to seek the God of his ancestor David at the age of 16. He chose as his ideal, not Amon, his father, or Manasseh, his grandfather, but "the man after God's own heart," his remote ancestor David.

With this power exerting itself in his life, Josiah became totally unlike his own father. By the time he was

20, he had begun a wholesale cleanup of his country, removing all traces of idol worship that had infested the Holy Land: altars, high places, images, groves, and priests.

He was just 26 when he launched his next program, the restoration of the temple. And there, in a dust-covered room, the Book of the Law of God was discovered.

In that lost and abandoned Word of the living God, Josiah found the picture of the better life he was seeking for himself and his people. In it he heard the approval of God on his kind of rule and the ideals he was following. In that Word he also found the power to break with the past and to stay with the new life. He was no longer Amon's son as much as he was God's, "having been born again, not of corruptible seed but of incorruptible, through the word of God which lives and abides forever" (1 Peter 1:23 NKJV).

By faith, Josiah improved on previous generations. As he swore allegiance to the King of heaven, he set a blessed course for his people. "And the king stood in his place and made a covenant before the LORD, to walk after the LORD and to keep His commandments and His testimonies and His statutes, with all his heart and all his soul, to perform the words of the covenant that were written in this book. ... And ... all his days they did not turn away from following the LORD the God of their fathers" (2 Chron. 34:31, 33).

One day Josiah died too. Again the familiar cry was heard in the land: The king is dead. Long live the king! Only this time "all Judah and Jerusalem mourned for Josiah" (2 Chron. 35:24), and generations lovingly recalled him and his fruitful reign in their songs and memorials.

JONAH

A man had two sons; and he went to the first and said, "Son, go and work in the vineyard today." And he answered, "I will not"; but afterward he repented and went.

Matt. 21:28–29 RSV

THE RELUCTANT PROPHET

SOMEHOW God's will gets done, if not by willing servants, then by reluctant ones. Like Jonah.

The mission God assigned to Jonah was an awesome one. Nineveh was known as "an exceedingly great city." Its population of perhaps more than 600,000 was large for those days. And the entire city was so drenched in wickedness that God threatened to overthrow it unless it repented. Jonah was selected by God to take that stern and unpopular message to the foreign capital. It was not an assignment the average man of God would covet.

Jonah as much as said no to God's command. When God ordered him to go eastward to preach judgment and repentance to Nineveh, Jonah went down to the Mediterranean Sea and booked passage on a ship going west to Tarshish. The voyage was no ticket seller's mistake. Jonah was determined to go "away from the presence of the LORD" (Jonah 1:3 RSV).

The next chapter of the story is familiar to everyone, Jonah was caught short as at the end of a leash. Via the large fish God had created for this purpose, Jonah was brought back to shore.

"Then the word of the LORD came to Jonah the second time, saying, 'Arise, go to Nineveh, that great city, and proclaim to it the message that I tell you.' So Jonah arose and went to Nineveh, according to the word of the LORD" (Jonah 3:1–3 RSV).

Entering the city boldly, Jonah cried the simple message of the Lord: "Yet forty days, and Nineveh shall be overthrown!" And, to his amazement (and regret!), the people of Nineveh believed God and repented, "from the greatest of them to the least of them" (Jonah 3:4–5 RSV).

And God spared the city gladly, delighting in its repentance.

The attitude of Jonah before and after his challenging mission cuts down his size in our eyes. And yet the mission he performed required heroism, boldness, and zeal. It is likely that Jonah learned, before God finished with him, that he himself was as much the object of God's patience and mercy as were the people to whom God sent him, and that Jonah himself needed to turn around in his flight away from God no less than the Ninevites needed to stop fleeing from God in their hearts.

At any rate, Jonah did finally say yes to the Lord's will, even though his first reaction was negative. He was like the first son in the story Jesus tells in Matthew 21: "A man had two sons; and he went to the first and said, 'Son, go and work in the vineyard today.' And he answered, 'I will not'; but afterward he repented and went. And he went to the second and said the same; and he answered, 'I go, sir,' but did not go. Which of the two did the will of his father?" (vv. 28–31 RSV). Obviously the first.

God would like to have His servants do His bidding willingly from the start; but He will settle for the latecomer who may have begun reluctantly and then did the will of the Father from the heart. Jesus assures us that there will be many "Jonahs" and "Bar-Jonas" (Son of Jonah) in the kingdom of God, while many who knew the will of the Father from earliest childhood will not enter the kingdom.

We pray: "Thy will be done on earth as it is in heaven." It is important that those who pray these words mean what they say and do that will. Although he began reluctantly, Jonah finally did that will.

Some become God's heroes because God will not take no for an answer.

ELIJAH

I have been very jealous for the LORD, the God of hosts.

1 Kings 19:14 RSV

AT THE BOTTOM OF THE BARREL

DAUNTLESS, bold, and fearless men. The world has seen many of them. They have ventured out against staggering odds to defend a cause, to liberate nations, or to make a name for themselves. Seldom, however, has there appeared in the cause of God a hero as striking as Elijah the Tishbite, who lived around 900 B. C. We must exhaust a thesaurus of synonyms to adequately describe the man.

There are times when God's cause demands a fearless champion. The reign of Ahab in Israel was one such time. Ahab was a powerful but evil ruler. Idolatry flourished in the land, and the king himself led the people in their drift away from the one true God.

Suddenly, like John the Baptist, God's latter-day Elijah, the prophet appeared in the wilderness. Having just informed Ahab that there would be neither dew nor rain for a long time, Elijah was commanded by God to hide in the desert region by the brook Cherith, and there the ravens (imagine!) would feed him. What did Elijah do with such a strange order? "He went and did according to the word of the LORD" (1 Kings 17:5). And there the greedy ravens brought bread and meat to God's man twice a day.

Soon the brook dried up. Now the prophet was subjected to another test. He was to travel to Sidon, a foreign country, and stay with a widow (imagine!) who was to feed him. Another strange command. But we read: "So he arose and went to Zarephath" (1 Kings 17:10). No questions, no excuses. Just obedience. When he arrived near the city, he found the widow getting ready to prepare her last meal for herself and her son. At the Lord's suggestion, Elijah demanded to be served the first part of this meal, and promised that the widow's food supply would not run out until the end of the drought.

Both Elijah and the widow had reached the bottom of the barrel. You may recall a certain type of children's bowl which has a picture on the bottom. You may have eaten from one yourself as a baby. The object is to get the child to eat up his cereal to see the picture on the bottom of the dish. Well, there was a picture of sorts at the bottom of the meal jar and oil cruse in the widow's house. It was an open hand of the Lord, and the legend read: "The Lord will refill." With his eyes of faith Elijah could see that picture there.

The widow, as if inspired by the faith of the prophet, "went and did as Elijah said; and she, and he, and her household ate for many days" (1 Kings 17:15). Panic and fear are contagious emotions. One terrified person in a crowd can set off a stampede or plunge the entire group into despair. On the other hand, one strong and fearless person can buoy up the hopes and spirits of many others. Elijah's faith was the combustible kind that ignited others to hope and believe.

We could go on to list numerous other situations in which the stalwart faith of God's man Elijah enabled him to face the wrath and whims of a bloody dictator, saw him through a one-man-plus-God challenge of 450 popular priests of Baal, and brought him unscathed to the floor of a flaming chariot that winged him out of this life and straight into heaven! Elijah had his lapses, his moments of frustration and despondency that come to all of the Lord's mighty warriors. But these passed as the word of the Lord sought out Elijah, lifted him up, and carried him along from wonder to wonder on the glorious road of faith.

Elijah ranks with John the Baptist as a forerunner of the Savior. His preaching was a bulldozer leveling the highway for the Messiah and a broom sweeping out hearts to prepare a throne room for the King of kings.

What fan, what fanatic, what zealot of the Lord would not desire a double portion of Elijah's spirit in a world far gone in dryness and hunger, fear and evil?

ELISHA

Then Elisha prayed and said, "O LORD, I Pray
Thee, open his eyes that he may see."

2 Kings 6:17a RSV

BELIEVING IS SEEING

ELISHA, God's bald and bold hero, seemed to have been finally backed into a corner.

The king of Syria (Ben-Hadad) was troubled because top secrets were leaking out of his palace to his enemy, the king of Israel. Tracking the leaks, he discovered it was Elisha, the prophet in Israel, who was to blame. "So he sent there [to Dothan] horses and chariots and a great army; and they came by night, and surrounded the city" (2 Kings 6:14). The bird that had been chirping out the secrets was trapped—or would be without much difficulty.

Early the next morning, Elisha's servant stepped out of the house and saw the Syrian army with horses and chariots round about the city. He ran trembling to Elisha and cried: "What shall we do?"

Unruffled at this turn of events, Elisha said: "Fear not, for those who are with us are more than those who are with them" (2 Kings 6:16 RSV).

The servant must have wondered: "Is he mad?

More with us than with them? How can there be? There's a whole army out there, blocking every way of escape; and there are just the two of us, a very unmilitary man of God and a terrified servant. Elisha must be seeing things!"

For a fact, Elisha *was* seeing things! What he "saw" kept him calm and unafraid. His faith had provided him with a vision of impenetrable protection. "Then Elisha prayed and said, 'O Lord, I pray Thee, open his eyes that he may see.' So the Lord opened the eyes of the young man, and he saw; and behold, the mountain was full of horses and chariots of fire round about Elisha" (2 Kings 6:17 RSV).

With his natural sight, Elisha could see no more than his servant. And to see that was enough to make any man walk out with his hands up, surrendering to superior forces. But Elisha had received a supernatural sight when he put his trust in the God of David, who had written some 100 years earlier: "I sought the Lord, and He answered me, and delivered me from all my fears. ... This poor man cried, and the Lord heard him, and saved him out of all his troubles. The angel of the Lord encamps around those who fear Him, and delivers them. O taste and see that the Lord is good! Happy is the man who takes refuge in Him!" (Ps. 34:4, 6–8 RSV).

God had placed the "fear extinguisher" near Elisha by giving him this promise of protection in the Psalms, and Elisha reached out for it and was saved in his troubles. Similar promises are situated by the loving Lord in every corner and at every turn of the believer's life. They need only to be reached.

The fiery angels and chariots were there surrounding Elisha and his servant all night long. The Syrian army could not move in on them so long as this inner circle of divine armor protected them. The eyes of God's believing children are privileged to see protection that unbelief can never see.

To demonstrate the Lord's control of the situation, the Syrian army was stricken with blindness, and in a later siege panicked in confusion at the sound of an invisible army.

Elisha's faith found the escape hatch in that tight corner in Dothan. He knew about it long before Paul wrote it out in 1 Cor. 10:13 RSV: "God is faithful, and He will not let you be tempted [tested] beyond your strength, but with the temptation [test] will also provide the way of escape, that you may be able to endure it."

NAAMAN'S WIFE'S MAID

Would that my lord were with the prophet who is in Samaria! He would cure him of his leprosy.

2 Kings 5:3 RSV

A SMALL AND NAMELESS WITNESS

GOD'S heroes and heroines come in all sizes. Some don't even have a name by which we might remember them. They leave behind them only the evidence of outstanding faith. One such anonymous little heroine was the captive maid of Naaman's wife.

This young Israelite girl, serving a general's wife in Syria, occupied a niche far below that of a child. Separated from her family and homeland, she was doomed to spend her life as a slave to strangers in a foreign land. Yet even there she was a child of God. She knew this. She cultivated the personal Father-daughter relationship God had established with her. She remembered the word of the Lord and was sustained by it in her nearly hopeless existence. No doubt she remembered to converse with her heavenly Father in prayer. At any rate, the Lord had not been wiped out of her memory or her daily thoughts. Though she was a mere maid, she was nevertheless a daughter of the King. Her Father-King was greater than her earthly master Naaman, who was just a general in the Syrian king's army.

The little girl loved God, and so she also loved her fellowman. You could tell it in her work. She was a faithful servant, sincerely anxious to be a good maid if that was what God wanted her to be. She soon won the respect and confidence of her master and mistress to the point where they were willing to listen to her opinion. It must have been evident to them that she loved them. She was concerned about their well-being. She wanted them to be physically and spiritually well.

Whether she was conscious of it or not, the little girl longed to have her master enjoy the security of God's family that she cherished. Even at her age she could see the emptiness in worshiping false gods. Without a course in comparative religion she knew the difference between the one, true, living God and those gods that people fashion for themselves, who, having eyes, see not, having ears, hear not, and having hands, cannot heal or help. There was One who sees and hears, helps and loves all. She knew Him. She would open her mouth at the risk of seeming impertinent, and she would offer Him to her leprous master Naaman. She decided what she would say to her mistress: "Would that my lord were with the prophet who is in Samaria! He would cure him of his leprosy."

Naaman, who had tried everything and despaired of ever being cured, clutched at this straw of hope. He sought out the prophet Elisha, learned that the maid was right, and finally was washed clean of his disease. More than that: he found the one true God at the end of the trail that began sometime earlier when God permitted a little girl of Israel to be carried off a captive in a Syrian border raid.

Now, who would think that a little girl, sweeping her master's house, attending her mistress, and running errands, might be carrying in her heart the key to a general's desperate problem, a leper's cure, and a sinner's cleansing? Would we imagine God would use such an instrument for so much good?

THE THREE
HEBREW CAPTIVES

*Blessed be the God of Shadrach, Meshach, and
Abednego, who has sent His angel and delivered
His servants, who trusted in Him, and set at
nought the king's command and yielded up their
bodies rather than serve and worship any god
except their own God.*

Dan. 3:28 RSV

TRY TO STOP US FROM WORSHIPING!

"THREE OFFICIALS DEFY ROYAL DECREE," the
headlines would have shouted in the Babylonian papers,
had there been newspapers in that land when Shadrach,
Meshach, and Abednego dared to resist the command of
King Nebuchadnezzar. The country was startled when
these three young Hebrew captives refused to obey the
king's order that everyone in the land worship his gold-
en image. Quickly the three were haled before the king
himself to answer for their defiance.

What they did would be somewhat similar to
three prominent government officials today going on
strike against the authorities for not being allowed to
worship as they please. Only with the three Hebrews

it was worse. They stood to lose not only their jobs, prominent and lucrative as they were, but they risked their very lives by insisting on their right to worship the only true God.

To think that there are people—young people—to whom worship—true worship—is so important! Amazing! Amazing today as it was then. In those days in Babylonia the average citizen was indifferent about the matter. If Nebuchadnezzar was the undisputed ruler and insisted that everybody perform a ritual giving him divine honor, they went along with the order. They could keep tongue in cheek. There was nothing for them to lose, and something to gain by obeying such a decree. And if, in a few years, Belshazzar, his son, would throw a party for a thousand nobles and use the sacred vessels of God's house for perverse heathen libations, why make an issue of it? Why upset the balance of things by objecting to religious theories? There is less agitation if you simply coast along with the prevailing system. And if, after the Babylonian Empire fades away, Darius the Mede forbids the worship of any god other than himself, how stupid for a prominent man like Daniel to resist the order and stake his life on the right to worship One he considers the true God!

In an age when worship is not decreed, when it is a matter of choice and more than half the population chooses to leave it alone, one would be quite surprised to see three men of the status of Shadrach, Meshach, and Abednego raising a fuss about worship. One might expect them to be utterly indifferent about the whole matter. It would be more natural for them to pose as blasé, sophisticated men-about-town who have more pressing or fascinating things to do than worship. Who gets worked up over the privilege of worshiping today? What odd minority would care whether there is a church to go to or not, and what the preacher is talking about? Churchgoing for many young people on the rise has little to offer the intellectual, little to challenge the questing spirit of the nation's budding leaders. It is for those who have nothing more engaging to do on Sunday morning, who have not outgrown the God of their childhood, who have no car to wash, no golf match to play, no Saturday night to recuperate from.

The three Judeans must have felt much different about worship and reverence for the one true God. To them freedom to worship was evidently as precious as any other freedom for which men are willing to stand their ground, resist, and even die. There is a connection with the Lord that can be maintained only by keeping open the lines of communication between God and man, and man and God. The word of the Lord must not be shut up, or man perishes. And when man stops speaking to God, he ends up madly babbling to himself or shouting into empty silence. The edict of Nebuchadnezzar threatened a possession which the Hebrews considered more precious than staying alive a few more years. They were willing to sacrifice this temporal life rather than lose their hold on the life they had found with the living God.

People say a great deal about their values by the prominence they give worship. God learns much about a person when the church bells ring.

NEHEMIAH

*Then I said to them, "You see the trouble we are in,
how Jerusalem lies in ruins with its gates burned.
Come, let us build the wall of Jerusalem, that we
may no longer suffer disgrace."*

Neh. 2:17 RSV

CLEANING UP SOMEONE ELSE'S MESS

WHAT do you do with a mess someone else has
made for you?

The situation that Nehemiah found on his return to
Palestine seemed almost hopeless. For more than two
generations the country had been practically stagnant.
The land of his fathers was in an advanced state of dete-
rioration. The thrones of Israel and Judah had been top-
pled, the temple plundered and destroyed, the walls
broken down, and the gates burned, the land pillaged
and neglected, and most of the nation led away captive
into far-off Babylonia. Only a remnant was left behind to
keep the land from going to complete waste. The people,
however, did not have their heart in their work. They
were toiling for foreign oppressors; their life was little
more than slavery. They would die and their children
too before there would be any hope of changing the conditions.

Out in Babylonia a captive Jew named Nehemiah enjoyed the comparative security of a palace position. He was butler to the king. Hearing a report of conditions in his homeland, Nehemiah was aroused to intercede for his people. The king permitted him to go back to Palestine with a group of exiles. When the band of displaced persons arrived in the Holy Land, they felt like crying. Everything was a shambles. Worse than that, no one seemed to care, no one seemed to be leading the people out of their distress, no one was pushing them to change the situation. With so little interest in correcting the mess, why should Nehemiah bother?

Furthermore, when Nehemiah determined to do something for the country, he ran into all kinds of opposition. He was ridiculed, factions became angry at him and sneered at him, plots were set up to cripple his plans; even his friends discouraged him and met his efforts with selfishness instead of sacrifice. Despite all this, Nehemiah forged ahead against all obstacles and indifference.

He was convinced that the work he was doing was the Lord's work. Injustice and oppression and neglect were signs to him that matters were not right. He was sure such conditions would disappear if the people returned to God and dedicated themselves to living His will. Though primarily a patriot and statesman interested in restoring order to the land and reestablishing the nation, Nehemiah constantly resorted to prayer. He consulted the Lord continually, as if He were an adviser at his elbow. Before speaking, he counseled with the Lord; before acting, he made sure he was following the Lord's directions.

A man of lesser faith might have thought, Why fix up something someone else has destroyed? Why help set up something for someone else when you may not live to enjoy it yourself? And when success doesn't come with the first or second effort, why not just give the whole mess a kick and walk away from it?

Nehemiah was the kind of national hero who begins picking up the pieces and starts putting them into some kind of order. Let someone else create the chaos. A follower of God, like God, will unremittingly set things in order, first between God and people, and then between people and people. God's people cannot sit still when there is housekeeping to be done in God's world.

MARY

Let it be to me according to Your word.
Luke 1:38 NKJV

A VESSEL OFFERED TO GOD

AT one time Mary looked forward to the average life of a poor Jewish housewife. Her fiancé was a carpenter, but this was no promise of wealth and luxury. If it were God's will, she would rear a family, and they would be a happy circle around their Nazareth hearth. That and little more could Mary expect when her life was suddenly and forever changed by the amazing visit of the Lord's angel.

Reaching from heaven after centuries of human history, the finger of the Lord God came to rest upon this unknown girl. Mary, of all the women in the world, would be the "blessed" one for all generations to come. In her wildest dreams she could not have imagined such honor and grace coming to her. She would be the instrument and vessel of God for the birth of the world's Redeemer. Those of low degree had been lifted up before. Mary could list any number of them in Jewish history. But who had ever been exalted like this? A Holy Thing would be born of her, a sinner! How could this be? Why should she be the mother of the Lord?

Overwhelmed by this appointment to destiny, Mary was humbled and awed. She could find in herself no reason why she should be so selected. How this was all part of God's plan! Mary tells about it in her magnificent song, the *Magnificat:*

> *My soul magnifies the Lord, and my spirit has rejoiced in God my Savior.*
>
> *For He has regarded the lowly state of His maidservant; for behold, henceforth all generations will call me blessed.*
>
> *For He who is mighty has done great things for me, and holy is His name.*
>
> *And His mercy is on those who fear Him from generation to generation.*
>
> *He has shown strength with His arm; He has scattered the proud in the imagination of their hearts.*
>
> *He has put down the mighty from their thrones, and exalted the lowly.*
>
> *He has filled the hungry with good things, and the rich He has sent empty away.*
>
> *He has helped His servant Israel, in remembrance of His mercy, as He spoke to our fathers, to Abraham and to his seed forever.*

(Luke 1:46–55 NKJV)

The song of Mary says many things about her.

This teenage maiden knew her Bible. Some scholars have found as many as 24 echoes of Old Testament Scripture in her brief song. The Messiah was no stranger to this poor girl. The expectation of the Savior enriched and filled her hungry life. She knew the faithful Lord would one day perform His promise, and the world would see its Savior.

What does a person like this do when God comes with such an offer of glory? She has nothing to offer but herself as a willing vessel of God. "Behold the maidservant of the Lord! Let it be to me according to Your word."

Was there ever another person in history like Mary, so blessed, so sought out by the Lord, so chosen to be His vessel? Her Son and God's Son says: " 'Who is My mother?' ... And He stretched out His hand toward His disciples and said, 'Here are My mother and My brothers! For whoever does the will of My Father in heaven is My brother and sister and *mother'* " (Matt. 12:48–50 NKJV [emphasis added]).

By the grace of God, Mary became the vessel of God and bore God's Son within her. By God's grace there are many Marys, equally precious to Him and equally honored by Him, who offer themselves to the Lord and are filled with His salvation. Blessed Mary! Blessed mothers of the Lord!

Simeon

Lord, now You are letting Your servant depart in peace, according to Your word.

Luke 2:29 NKJV

Standing at the End of the Line

MANY of God's heroes appear in their young and vigorous years. They show their faith in a heroic feat or burst of action under tremendous odds. Their very youth makes them impatient with the past and with the status quo. They can hardly wait to correct the mistakes made by their forefathers. So heroism is often the medal on a young man's chest.

However, not all of God's heroes were pioneers or trailblazers. Some, like aged Anna and Simeon, stood at the end of the line, growing old as they waited for the fulfillment of God's promises. Their confidence does not appear in the divine record as the explosion of a supernova in the skies, but as a steadily glowing star, flickering its light night after night in the world's deep darkness. This is not easy. Most would prefer the single bold action to the long, long wait. Simeon waited and waited and waited.

The Bible pictures Simeon as that just and devout man in Jerusalem "waiting for the Consolation of Israel.

... And it had been revealed to him by the Holy Spirit that he would not see death before he had seen the Lord's Christ" (Luke 2:25–26 NKJV).

God had made a rare promise to Simeon. Thousands upon thousands before him had the same hope of seeing with the eyes of their flesh the fulfillment of God's great promise of salvation. Simeon was one of the rare, blessed ones whose eyes were privileged to witness the Lord's first coming. "Blessed are the eyes which see what you see!" Jesus told His contemporaries. "For I tell you that many prophets and kings desired to see what you see, and did not see it, and to hear what you hear, and did not hear it" (Luke 10:23, 24 RSV). God promised Simeon that he would be one of those fortunate persons.

One day it finally came about. That day the Spirit of God led Simeon to the temple (what better place to find God's promised Word?) and while he was there, a poor couple, people of the working class, entered, carrying a Baby. Simeon approached them, took the Child into his own arms, blessed God, and spoke the Nunc Dimittis: "Lord, now You are letting Your servant depart in peace, according to Your word; for my eyes have seen Your salvation" (Luke 2:29, 30 NKJV).

Now his life was complete. He had arrived at the point for which he had been born and loved by God, and for which God had prepared His Salvation. He was through waiting. Now he could depart in peace. In his arms he held the cancellation of all his debts, the fulfilling of all his deficiencies, and all the light that he needed to cross the dark river of death. There, in a little bundle, was the love and Word of God made flesh. It could be held and embraced, received and treasured. It could be seen and felt. It was real. It was worth waiting for, no matter how many long and dreary years.

With this experience another word of Christ applied to Simeon: "The last shall be first, and the first last." Seemingly at the end of the line of Old Testament waiters, Simeon is one of the very first in the line of New Testament witnesses of the Savior. And he is in the lengthy glorious list of God's heroes as proof that God's promises are fulfilled for those who wait Him out.

THE WISE MEN

Where is He who has been born King of the Jews?
Matt. 2:2 RSV

WISE MEN IN SEARCH OF A KING

ALL the preparations had been checked and double-checked. Each of the distinguished travelers was ready. They would leave together the very next day. The caravan would be equipped for a long journey. It might be months before they returned, if they could be sure of returning at all. Travel was dangerous in those days, especially for wealthy people.

But they were determined to go anyway. They didn't know how far they would be traveling. That would be up to the star. It had appeared in the heavens, and it was on the move. Westward.

They were known as wise men. But, to all appearances, they looked foolish setting out after a moving star, like simpletons pursuing the rainbow to find the pot of gold at its end. They might not look so wise if their calculations proved to be wrong. They would look quite silly coming back home, poorer but much wiser. They could still change their mind and stay home. They could let the star go on without them.

But were their calculations off? They had done

their research painstakingly. They had followed carefully the directions of the most reliable guide they
could find. There it had been written: "There shall
come a Star out of Jacob, and a Scepter shall rise out of
Israel" (Num. 24:17). This meant that the arrival of a
great king would be marked by a special star. In their
study of the skies they recognized the new star and
made their decision. They would seek out the King
whose coming was proclaimed by the heavens. They
counted themselves fortunate to be living when this
long-awaited event was taking place. Hundreds of
years before, their ancestors had heard about the One
who was to come from the Jewish nation, then captive.
Daniel and his countrymen had boldly and openly
proclaimed the true God who would someday send
the world its Messiah. Somehow this prophecy had
gotten into the hands of the Wise Men, and now they
were about to have a part in the great drama.

They were more than just curious about what was
happening. They had more than an objective scientific
interest in the heavenly phenomenon. They were sure
that the Dayspring (the Morning Star) from on high was
about to visit mankind sitting in midnight darkness. The
appearance of the star convinced them that the ancient
promise was true. The Creator of the star was sending
the newborn King. They were prepared to kneel before
Him, Baby that He was, and worship Him.

There was no more time to lose. Their houses
must be set in order before their departure. Someone
must take charge of their affairs while they are gone,
and take over for them should they not return. And
gifts had to be prepared, royal gifts, for the infant

King. No detail was overlooked.

The journey began. Finally they arrived in Jerusalem. Straight to the palace they went and asked their question: "Where is the King?" Not: "Is there a King?" but, "Where is He who has been born the King of the Jews?" It wasn't the right place. That nameplate belonged not in Herod's palace, but over a stable and later on a cross. But they were on the track. There was such a King. They would just have to travel a little farther before they found Him. The exact place of His birth was Bethlehem, not Jerusalem. A slight correction in their directions, another look at the star, and they were on their way.

Yes, they would find Him. The seekers would locate the Seeker, and both would be happy to have found each other.

John the Baptist

I tell you, among those born of women none is greater than John.

Luke 7:28 RSV

None Greater

MANY in the days of Jesus were making big head-lines in the world. Roman emperors were shaping events and nations. Writers were recording for the ages immortal prose, poetry, and drama. Sculptors were fashioning masterpieces in stone. Architects were designing structures that awe us to this day. The military were forging invincible forces. Scientists were busy making far-reaching discoveries. Doctors and philosophers were gaining new insights into the body and mind of man. It was a rich and lively age. Some even left their names in history as men and women who knew how to outdo all previous generations in devising special pleasures.

And in a desert, next to a crooked river running through a corner of the world, a young man, about 30 years old, was gathering crowds of curiosity-seekers to hear his strange message: "Make straight the way of the Lord" (John 1:23 RSV). It was a peculiar message from a peculiar man. He was dressed in camel's hair, and he fed on locusts and wild honey. The message contained more.

He pointed to Jesus passing by and cried: "Behold, the Lamb of God, who takes away the sin of the world!" (John 1:29 RSV).

His ministry did not last long. His scene on the stage of history was brief. It was cut short when he criticized the puppet king of Palestine, was thrown into prison, and then was beheaded during the king's wild birthday party. A few of John's followers buried his body, and that would have been the last trace of him, except ... except that Jesus said: "I tell you, among those born of women none is greater than John."

He must have had reasons for saying so. We all have our measurements for greatness. Some use the yardstick of power or accomplishments or beauty or service or the number of lines a celebrity rates in *Who's Who*. Wouldn't it be interesting to know how God measures greatness?

A few of His standards come readily to mind: "He [God] does not delight in the strength of the horse; He takes no pleasure in the legs of a man. The LORD takes pleasure in those who fear Him, in those who hope in His mercy" (Ps. 147:10–11 NKJV). "But on this one will I look: on him who is poor and of a contrite spirit, and who trembles at My word" (Is. 66:2 NKJV). "You know that the rulers of the Gentiles lord it over them, and their great men exercise authority over them. It shall not be so among you; but whoever would be great among you must be your servant, and whoever would be first among you must be your slave; even as the Son of Man came not to be served but to serve, and to give His life as a ransom for many" (Matt. 20:25–28 RSV).

John lived by the motto: "He [Jesus] must increase, but I must decrease" (John 3:30). To him, Christ was the Bridegroom, he himself was just one of the attendants at the wedding. The finger of his life and words was not pointed at himself, but at Him whose shoelaces John did not feel worthy to untie. John knew that "He who comes from above is above all" (John 3:31). He was determined not to diminish the light of God's Son by letting the shadow of his own personality stand in front of it. When people were looking for their life and their peace, he would not permit his head to be in the way. He would lower himself so they could see Jesus standing above him.

It looks as if we must revise our list of history's greats. The mighty men of old will have to step down and let this "prophet" occupy the first place. "A prophet? Yes, I tell you, and more than a prophet. This is he of whom it is written, 'Behold, I send My messenger before Thy face, who shall prepare Thy way before Thee'" (Luke 7:26–27 RSV). This very last herald of the Savior, Jesus places at the head of the list.

But this isn't the end of the sentence. The whole of it goes like this: "I tell you, among those born of women none is greater than John; yet he who is least in the kingdom of God is greater than he." That could be you—or I!

THE TENTH LEPER

*Then one of them, when he saw that he was healed,
turned back, praising God with a loud voice; and he
fell on his face at Jesus' feet, giving Him thanks.
Now he was a Samaritan.*

Luke 17:15–16 RSV

IN SICKNESS AND IN HEALTH

A HERO of World War II distinguished himself
valiantly in battle. After the war, as a civilian, he lost the
battle of the bottle. In war he was a hero, in peace a failure.

In their dreadful illness 10 lepers had learned to
pray and where to look for help. As Jesus came by, they
cried to the Lord of might and mercy: "Have pity on us."
Who wouldn't pity the poor wretches? Separated from
health and family and society, they lived a living death.
No malady was more dreaded in those days than leprosy. Only rarely was it cured. Most victims could expect
to remain lepers until they died. No wonder the lepers
who caught Jesus passing by begged Him to have mercy
on them.

And Jesus answered their prayer, providing them
with the precious gift they desired: health.

Suddenly the need for Christ vanished. He was a

foulweather friend, and they had just stepped out of the storm into the sunshine of glowing health. There was so much lost time to make up, so many things to do. They hurried off in all directions, each to resume his own life. Now they could get along without Jesus. Who needs a doctor when he isn't sick? They would keep Him in mind if they possibly needed Him again.

One of them, however, stops in his tracks, looks again at his restored body, blinks his eyes in amazement, and immediately turns around to locate the Giver of this precious gift. All the rest can wait. He has a debt to repay, and a mere thank you will hardly do. But he must at least say thanks.

The man has no name. But he does have a tag. He is a Samaritan. And this makes his reaction all the more unusual. It was normal behavior for Samaritans to look down or askance upon the Jews. And Jesus was a Jew. Anything the Jews had, the Samaritans felt they could match or exceed. They wanted to owe nothing to the Jews, from whom they had separated centuries before. The "normal" Samaritan reaction to Jesus would have been: "Take what He can give you, but don't lower yourself before Him, don't place yourself under obligation to Him." We are impressed by the Samaritan's response because he overcomes this impulse to behave in a normal Samaritan manner.

Besides, he overcomes the hazard of good health. Sickness makes pray-ers and beggars out of many who would not otherwise turn their thoughts upward. It is easy to do without God when one's body is functioning perfectly. One can go for years without feeling the need of God, and since good health seems to be a sign that all's well with the world, feelings of guilt do not seem to send the healthy person hunting for a Savior.

The healed lepers were still sinners even though their health was restored. The granting of health was not a sign that their sins were forgiven. They were still creatures of God even though they were no longer outcasts of the community. And the fact that they were members of God's chosen race made them no less needful of the Messiah whom God was sending the world through their nation. But all this seemed normal. They felt they had this coming to them. They would have felt cheated if they didn't have this normal life. After all, didn't others enjoy good health and spiritual blessings without getting down on their knees each day to beg for them?

The Samaritan ex-leper met the test of health as well as he met the test of illness. He passed the test of prosperity as well as he passed the test of adversity. In sickness and in health, his faith stayed anchored in the same Rock.

"He turned back, praising God with a loud voice." If he could cry out in misery, could he keep silent in joy? "And he fell on his face at Jesus' feet, giving Him thanks." Who else deserved the credit for making him whole?

Jesus, seeing this one-out-of-ten response, said to him, "Rise and go your way; your faith has made you well" (Luke 17:19 RSV). The other nine were still sick with a fatal illness. This one was healed forever.

THE CENTURION

Truly, I say to you, not even in Israel have I found such faith.

Matt. 8:10 RSV

TABLE SPACE FOR A FOREIGN SOLDIER

THE streets of Capernaum, our Lord's headquarters during His Galilean ministry, often shook to the thunder of marching feet. The city near the Sea of Galilee harbored a Roman garrison. It was not at all unusual to run into soldiers and officers anywhere in town.

The Jews, whose country was occupied by the mighty Romans, had learned to live with the situation, as much as they resented it. And the soldiers, because of their special mission, had little to do with the Jews, whom they despised. Prejudices against foreigners and minorities were as strong then as they are today.

The Lord, however, drew no boundary lines. He had come to seek and to save that which was lost. And all were lost, Jew and Roman alike. He came to bring light to those sitting in darkness. And all were in darkness. He came to bring life to the dead. And all were "dead in trespasses and sins." He came to reconcile those who had become God's enemies and had lost His peace. And all were captives of the devil until

Jesus took captivity captive.

Somehow a centurion, a captain in the Roman army, learned this about Jesus. And through his uniform, through his alien nationality, the grace of God penetrated, and his allegiance was shifted to a higher Ruler. This soldier found salvation among the Jews and even built a synagog for them in Capernaum.

This centurion is a remarkable man in many ways. He represents one of the early trophies won by Christ out of the pagan world. His faith is demonstrated by one virtue after another. Instead of the expected callousness of the typical Roman soldier (such as those who tortured and mocked Jesus before His crucifixion), this officer was moved by love and sympathy for his servant, of all people! The servant was likely a Jew. At any rate, to the ordinary Roman he was just a slave, a piece of property. One didn't usually waste sympathy on slaves or become disturbed by their suffering. Slaves were meant to suffer. But this centurion contradicts all expectations. He is sorry for his paralyzed and suffering servant. He wants to do everything he can to help him.

The centurion searched out Jesus and pleaded with Him to do something for the servant. He calls Jesus "Lord." Here was another break with his pagan background. If anyone was lord to a Roman, it was one of many gods, or the emperor. To the centurion, Jesus of Nazareth, of the despised Jewish race, was the Lord. This is not just a title of respect, but a recognition of Jesus as the Savior. The centurion believed that Jesus could do for him and his servant what neither Roman gods nor emperor could do. Besides, he felt unworthy in the presence of Jesus. Something must have changed in him: a

Roman unworthy in the presence of a Jew!

"The Jews seek a sign," says Paul, analyzing a peculiar characteristic of his people. But so do many others who demand some special evidence that the power of God is operating. The centurion brushed aside all such crutches for his faith. He said: "Lord, I am not worthy to have You come under my roof; but only say the word, and my servant will be healed. For I am a man under authority, with soldiers under me; and I say to one, 'Go,' and he goes, and to another, 'Come,' and he comes, and to my slave, 'Do this,' and he does it" (Matt. 8:8–9 RSV). This kind of faith Jesus had never before witnessed. "When Jesus heard him, He marveled, and said to those who followed Him, 'Truly, I say to you, not even in Israel have I found such faith' " (v. 10).

And then He pointed to some empty chairs that are set around the King's table in heaven, and said that they would be occupied by people like the centurion from the east and the west, and they would sit next to Abraham, Isaac, and Jacob. It was wonderful when the Jews who were anticipating the Messiah for centuries recognized Him when He came and believed in Him. But when a Gentile soldier had eyes to see the Lord's Christ, this was enough to make Jesus Himself marvel!

THE MAN BORN BLIND

One thing I know, that though I was blind, now I see.

John 9:25 RSV

THE UNSHAKABLE WITNESS

SCENE 1: (*The man born blind and his neighbors*)

First neighbor: Is not this the man who used to sit and beg?

Second neighbor: It is he.

Others: No, but he is like him.

The man born blind: I am the man.

First neighbor: Then how were your eyes opened?

The man born blind: The man called Jesus made clay and anointed my eyes and said to me, "Go to Siloam and wash"; so I went and washed and received my sight.

Second neighbor: Where is He?

The man born blind: I do not know.

SCENE 2: (*The man born blind is brought to the Pharisees.*)

First Pharisee: Now tell us, how did you receive your sight?

The man born blind: He put clay on my eyes, and I washed, and I see.

Second Pharisee: When did this happen?

The man born blind: On the last Sabbath day.

Second Pharisee: This man is not from God, for He does not keep the sabbath.

First Pharisee: How can a man who is a sinner do such signs?

Second Pharisee: What do you say about Him, since He has opened your eyes?

The man born blind: He is a prophet.

SCENE 3: (*The parents of the man born blind are questioned by the Pharisees and the Jews.*)

The Jews: Is this your son, who you say was born blind? How then does he now see?

The Parents (*evasively, for fear of being excommunicated from the synagog if they confess Jesus to be the Christ*): We know that this is our son, and that he was born blind; but how he now sees we do not know, nor do we know who opened his eyes. Ask him; he is of age, he will speak for himself.

SCENE 4: (*The Jews and Pharisees recall the man born blind for further questioning.*)

The Jews: Give God the praise; we know that this man is a sinner.

The man born blind: Whether He is a sinner, I do not know; one thing I know, that though I was blind, now I see.

The Jews: What did He do to you? How did He

open your eyes?

The man born blind: I have told you already, and you would not listen. Why do you want to hear it again? Do you too want to become His disciples?

The Pharisees (*mockingly*): You are *His* disciple, but we are disciples of Moses. We know that God has spoken to Moses, but as for this man, we do not know where He comes from.

The man born blind: Why, this is a marvel! You do not know where He comes from, and yet He opened my eyes. We know that God does not listen to sinners, but if any one is a worshiper of God and does His will, God listens to him. Never since the world began has it been heard that any one opened the eyes of a man born blind. If this man were not from God, He could do nothing.

The Pharisees: You were born in utter sin, and would you teach us? (And they cast him out.)

SCENE 5: (*Jesus and the man born blind*)

Jesus: Do you believe in the Son of God?

The man born blind: And who is He, sir, that I may believe in Him?

Jesus: You have seen Him, and it is He who speaks to you.

The man born blind: Lord, I believe.

Jesus: For judgment I came into this world, that those who do not see may see, and that those who see may become blind.

(Quoted from John 9 RSV)

THE SINFUL WOMAN

She loved much.

Luke 7:47

NO MORE IMITATION LOVE

THE invitation stated, "Dinner is served at the appointed hour." Jesus presented Himself at the door of the Pharisee's house, entered, and sat down at the table.

The meal had just begun when a woman with a bad reputation in town came into the house uninvited, holding in her hands an expensive jar of perfume, and weeping. In shocked silence the host watched what she did next. She came behind Jesus and let her tears fall on His feet. Then she dried them with her hair and anointed them with the perfume. Speechless, the Pharisee thought: "If this man were a prophet, He would have known who and what sort of woman this is who is touching Him, for she is a sinner" (Luke 7:39 RSV).

For all his close watching, the Pharisee saw only a corrupt woman polluting his house with her presence, imposing on his hospitality. Besides, he was a little disappointed in Jesus. He had considered Jesus a prophet, a preacher of righteousness, a man who holds virtue and godliness in high regard. All at once he felt he was the holiest one in the room. He did not see that he and the woman were both in need of the same thing, the thing both of them were seeking and for which they were finding only substitutes.

Like everyone else, the Pharisee and the woman were looking for love. They wanted to be loved. But they were mistaken about love. They were accepting substitutes and counterfeits. The Pharisee confused love with recognition and praise. He wanted others, including Jesus, to think highly of him. He was even willing to spend the price of a dinner to obtain this kind of approval. His paying for that approval was calculated. He felt the dinner invitation was enough for now. There was no need for him to greet Jesus enthusiastically or to offer Him a basin of water to wash the dust off His feet. He would invest no more in this dinner than he had to. There was the possibility that Jesus might let him down—and He surely did.

The woman had also been looking for love for a long time, perhaps since childhood. Many women with her kind of reputation are desperately clutching at any semblance of love. They too are often deceived by imitation love. They think it can be found in a function of the body, an emotional thrill, a flattering word. But what she peddled and what others bought was not love after all. The fairy tales and novels and popular songs called it love, but it was really something else. The love she knew was also calculated and bartered and paid for in one way or another.

One day the sinful woman, who had in her way "loved" much, met Him who loved genuinely, divinely.

He had nothing to gain for Himself by offering her the love of God. One day those feet she was washing and kissing and anointing would be nailed to a cross for her many corruptions. Here was love, not that she had loved God, but that God had loved her and gave His only Son to be the atonement for her sins.

She found love when she found Jesus, for Jesus showed her the heart of God, which is love. The more she saw of that love, the more grateful she felt, and the more she loved God in return.

The Pharisee held on to his counterfeit love, which was really a love of himself. He felt little need for forgiveness, and none for faith in his holy Guest. And so he loved little.

The bad woman found love when she found forgiveness, and she found both when she found Christ. By these steps she crawled out of the gutter into the clean and holy and happy family of God: by Christ, by forgiveness, by faith, and by love. Such people go into the kingdom of God ahead of the Pharisees.

THE WIDOW OF THE MITES

She out of her poverty put in all that she had, her whole livelihood.

Mark 12:44 NKJV

MORE THAN AN OFFERING

THE call to worship has sounded. In homes throughout the city, young and old of every class are preparing to visit the Lord's house. First the dressing up in the best clothes, then the calling together of the family, then a last look around that nothing has been forgotten. Oh, yes, remember to take along an offering!

In one of those homes, a poor one, a lonely widow is going through the same preparations. She may stop to wonder whether she should go this day at all. She is down to her last two mites. Together, the two coins are hardly worth picking up off the table. They can scarcely purchase a sacrifice to be offered in the temple by the priest. Besides, there would be other worshipers in the temple who would be better dressed than she. Out of their surplus they would be able to contribute more than she has to her name. She could certainly use those two mites for her own needs. Tomorrow the stores would be open again, and she would be hungry. She could buy a little food with the mites, enough to make a last meal before she would be completely dependent on others.

But she was "hungry" now, and the temple of God was open. There she could picture the Bread of Life waiting to feed her, and the Water of Life which satisfies. Had not God said: "Man shall not live by bread alone, but man lives by every word that proceeds from the mouth of the LORD"? (Deut. 8:3 NKJV). Sooner or later she would have to invest those two mites in food, and then they would be gone. Suppose she decided to give up that food and make a last sacrifice instead. Had not God been opening His hands to feed her until now? It would be little enough to show Him how much she appreciated His goodness and trusted Him for the next day's cares.

Who knows what she thought, the nameless widow of the two mites, as she closed the door of her house and walked up Zion to the temple? We might as well imagine that she went through no mental torture trying to decide how much of an offering to contribute that day or whether to go to church at all. For all we know, her casting of all her money into the treasury may have been done all in one motion as part of a life moving with everything it has in the direction of God.

The widow may not have known it, but she was involved in a crucial decision. Not only the rich are tempted by money. So are the poor. The rich are inclined to make it everything in their life because they have it. But the poor can make it everything in their life too, simply because they do not have it and are always worrying about it. The rich man can delude himself into thinking that he has done all that is necessary if he has given something to God and to charity. And yet the giving may not have deprived him of any comfort or luxury or caused him any loss. The poor man, on the other hand, may excuse himself from doing anything at all in the way of service to God or his fellowman by pleading poverty, as if to say: "You prevented me from doing anything, Lord, because You made me so poor."

At offering time in the service, the widow's mites outranked much larger sums falling into the treasury that day. Many of the others were merely leftovers; hers was a sacrifice. In the church treasurer's books her coins hardly made it to the decimal point. But in God's book they put many others to shame.

THE SYROPHOENICIAN WOMAN

Then Jesus answered her, "O woman, great is your faith!"

Matt. 15:28 RSV

A TREASURE NOT TO BE LOST

USUALLY Jesus is pictured in the Scriptures as the Seeker. He is the Good Shepherd hunting for the one lost sheep. He is the King sending His messengers into the highways and byways to invite all to His great supper so that every single remaining place at His table is occupied. No one can mistake His personal interest in every human being, an interest so intense that each can say, "Christ died for *me* and gave Himself for *me*."

On one occasion, however, our Lord seems to step out of character. We find Him retiring for a while in the foreign regions of Tyre and Sidon. There "He entered a house, and would not have anyone know it; yet He could not be hid" (Mark 7:24 RSV). He wished to remain incognito, for reasons not revealed. But He could not be hid, anymore than a candle on a stick or a city on a hill. Especially to someone who was searching for Him as diligently as was the Canaanite woman of Syrophoenicia.

Pleading for her demon-possessed daughter, she came to Jesus. She knew Him to be more than a passing charlatan, a fly-by-night faith healer. She called Him by a name that acknowledged Him for what He was: the Son of David. And she called Him Lord. Put these two names together and you have the equivalent of Messiah, or Savior. It was the Savior, coming from the nation and lineage of David, in whom this Canaanite woman was putting her trust for help. She knew that He would be able to cast the devil out of her child, for He had come into the world to destroy the works of the devil.

It is here that we run across one of the strangest remarks ever heard from the lips of the loving Savior. "I was sent only to the lost sheep of the house of Israel." It was as though He were deliberately brushing her off. But she would not be discouraged. She made her way past the circle of disciples, who resented being pestered by her. Like a puppy at the heels of its master, she kept coming, begging for attention. "Lord, help me!" she cried.

Again Jesus answered: "It is not fair to take the children's bread and throw it to the dogs." He meant that the feast of salvation was prepared on the table of the Jewish nation. Their seats were set around the table first. The Savior had come to their nation, to their land, spoke their language, and bore the name of their God, Immanuel. Still the woman would not be put off. She came back with the reply: "Yes, Lord, yet even the dogs eat the crumbs that fall from their master's table."

The woman had caught sight of a treasure to be coveted, something so rich that it overflows the table on which it stands. It was already in the hands of God's chosen people, but she desired some of it too. She didn't want it taken away from them to be given to her; she would be satisfied with the leftovers.

Jesus, in delaying His response to her, was testing her hold on the treasure. How much did she really want it? Would ridicule later make her release her grasp of it? Suppose people said to her: What do you want with that Jewish salvation? Our Phoenician culture and religion are superior or at least every bit as good. Why do you lower yourself to associate with those people who once tried to wipe out our ancestors?

She stayed with the test till it was over. She kept knocking at the door of the Kingdom which is for all, Jew and Gentile alike. When Jesus saw her confirmed in her decision, He welcomed her with a rare sentence of commendation. He who can detect faith the size of a mustard seed said to this woman: "Great is your faith!"

She had persisted long enough to learn that "every one who asks receives, and he who seeks finds, and to him who knocks it will be opened" (Matt. 7:8 RSV).

JOHN

Hereby perceive we the love of God, because He laid down His life for us; and we ought to lay down our lives for the brethren.

1 John 3:16

THUNDER AND LOVE

"BOANERGES" Jesus nicknamed John and his brother James. "Sons of Thunder" was a fitting description of the two at the time they were called to be disciples. Even after they had been following Christ for a while, the flashes of temper were still there. When a village of Samaritans would not welcome Jesus, their Master, James and John said to Jesus: " 'Lord, do You want us to command fire to come down from heaven and consume them, just as Elijah did?' But He turned and rebuked them, and said, 'You do not know what manner of spirit you are of. For the Son of Man did not come to destroy men's lives but to save them' " (Luke 9:54–56 NKJV).

James and John were not only impatient. They were driven for a time by a consuming ambition to lord it over others, to acquire the first and second places in the coming kingdom of Christ. Their mother backed them up in this request, interceding for them before Jesus. Though the Lord admired zeal and persistence in people, He would not coddle or excuse anger and ambition in His disciples.

As John (and his brother) stayed on with Jesus, he came more and more under the Lord's warming influence. By and by, Boanerges was no longer an apt picture of John's nature. Eventually that name was replaced by the enviable appellation "the disciple whom Jesus loved." The zeal was still there, but it was no longer squandered in short-fused blowups. Now it was channeled into the steadily flowing exercise of love. Of all the disciples, John became the closest to Jesus. This was inevitable as he resembled more and more the nature of his Lord.

Faith meets many challenges. One of the most difficult, so as to be almost impossible, is to love others. Love is the fulfilling of the Law, the performance of God's will. And we know that no one can do this to the complete satisfaction of God. Our keeping of the commandments breaks down in the area of love. To be able to love perfectly would be to be equal with God, for God is Love. The more godly a person becomes, the more loving he is. Love distinguishes between the believer and the unbeliever, between the saved and the lost, between true godliness and hypocrisy. Without love, even dying for one's faith and feeding the poor and being expert in religious knowledge are worth nothing (See 1 Cor. 13).

Love is truly a difficult virtue. It borders on the heroic, especially when it reaches out to embrace one's enemy and prays for one's persecutor. Love is just as difficult to exercise within the family, between children, between children and parents, and vice versa. There must have been family squabbles in John's family in their early years, what with the quick tempers and the competition for supremacy. But this gave way as love took over. John must have learned the power and technique of love from Christ very well. He was the logical one to be entrusted with the care of our Lord's mother, Mary, as Jesus died on the cross. And it isn't too hard to imagine Mary in her declining years catching frequent glimpses of her divine Son in John as she saw love growing and glowing in him.

To John, this part of Christian faith was to be valued most highly. His letters exalt the love of God in Christ and urge the reader to reflect God's love in all human relations.

As John increased in love, he soared higher and higher and moved in the lofty companionship of God. The eagle is a good symbol for John. The disciple of love was blessed with special insight and depth and visions, and lived in the closest possible communion with his Lord.

It's a long way from thunder to love—but faith can bridge the gap. It did for John.

ZACCHAEUS

Blessed are the pure in heart, for they shall see God.
Matt. 5:8

A CROOK GOES STRAIGHT

ZACCHAEUS (meaning *"Pure"*)! What a name for a chief tax collector! Especially in the days of Jesus, when publicans had a reputation for being crooked.

"Zacchaeus!" You can imagine his countrymen sneering as he passed by. *"Pure, justified."* Hah! A better name for him would be "sinner, crook, oppressor, traitor." It was bad enough that they were under the foreign rule of the Romans. It was worse that one of their own nation should collect taxes for the Romans. If a man went so far to make a living, he was not beyond squeezing the taxpayers for a little extra to fatten his commission. Zacchaeus, says Luke, was a chief tax collector, and rich. It figured.

Doors did not open readily to this little man. His reputation went ahead of him, and people learned to greet him with suspicion. Many a person walked away from an encounter with Zacchaeus cut and bleeding financially. When Zacchaeus confronted a taxpayer, it was to take, and sometimes to take more than he should. He had the law on his side, and he knew where the loopholes were if he needed them.

One day, for who knows what reason, Zacchaeus wanted to see Jesus who happened to be passing through Jericho. It must have been the prompting of the Holy Spirit that created this urge in him. It could not have been any financial consideration. Jesus was of the poorest of the poor, and, besides, he paid His taxes elsewhere—in Capernaum (Matt. 17:24–27). Zacchaeus could not expect to grow rich financially by making the acquaintance of Jesus. Nevertheless "he sought to see who Jesus was, but could not, on account of the crowd, because he was small of stature. So he ran on ahead and climbed up into a sycamore tree to see Him, for He was to pass that way" (Luke 19:3–4 RSV).

Jesus, walking by the tree, looked up and said to him: "Zacchaeus, make haste and come down; for I must stay at your house today." And Zacchaeus, overjoyed at the friendly self-invitation of Jesus, welcomed Him into his house, which saw very few voluntary visitors.

Sometime during that encounter with Jesus, Zacchaeus came to faith. And when he did, a strange and marvelous transformation took place in him. The taker turned into a giver. Greed was replaced by generosity. "Zacchaeus stood there and said to the Lord, 'Here and now, sir, I give half my possessions to charity; and if I have cheated anyone, I am ready to repay him four times over' " (Luke 19:8 NEB). If Zacchaeus had undergone such a change of heart and habit as a young child, it would not have been so amazing. But for a man advanced in years, accustomed to wealth and hardened to small and great injustices, to make such an about-face—this is evidence of some tremendous force operating in him.

Clearly, Zacchaeus had moved out of the center of his own life, and Christ had moved into it. The spiritually stunted man began to grow unbelievably tall. By the visit and influence of Jesus the name of Zacchaeus began to fit him. By the grace of God the impure and unjust man became pure and justified. By the mercy of God, Zacchaeus was privileged to catch Jesus on His last journey through Jericho, going to the tree waiting for Him in Jerusalem. Zacchaeus had to get up into a tree to see his Salvation. Jesus had to mount a tree so the Zacchaeuslike, materially possessed world would have no excuse for missing its Salvation.

Zacchaeus. For this man it was no longer a misnomer. He was Zacchaeus in fact. And he knew what Jesus meant when He said: "Blessed are the pure in heart, for they shall see God" (Matt. 5:8). Zacchaeus had seen Jesus and so had seen God (John 12:45) and found the blessedness of the pure in heart.

BARTIMAEUS

And Jesus said to him, "Go your way; your faith has made you well."

Mark 10:52 RSV

"... THE BLIND SEE ..."

BARTIMAEUS was accustomed to being silenced. People eventually got tired of hearing him plead for alms. It didn't help to throw him a coin one day. He was there with his hand outstretched again the next day. Blind Bartimaeus could hear some footsteps making a wide circle around his roadside station. He could almost sense them turning away their eyes so that they would not have to see the sightless wretch. It spoiled their day to find this blotch of abnormality sitting in their work-ward or playward or homeward path. If only he would keep quiet and resign himself to his fate! Who could help him? No doctor was known to cure such ailments. He was stuck with his tragedy. If he would just stop inflicting his misery on others, stop making them feel guilty and helpless.

Now once again "many rebuked him, telling him to be silent." It was embarrassing for the multitude striding along with Jesus out of Jericho to have the town's beggar disrupting the mood. "But he cried out all the more: 'Son of David, have mercy on me!' " (Mark 10:48 RSV). He couldn't keep quiet this time. Jesus was passing by! He had to catch the ear of Jesus. This was the only person who could help him. And He might not come this way again. "Jesus, Son of David, have mercy on me!" came the wail from his hoarse throat.

And Jesus heard. Bartimaeus knew it was really Jesus by the way He responded to the cry. Jesus stopped and said: "Call him." His heart began to pound faster as he was told that Jesus was calling him. How like the Jesus he had heard so much about! Merciful, kind, sympathetic. At least He cared enough to stop.

Bartimaeus threw off his mantle at once, jumped up, and groped his way to Jesus. Now the tension was almost unbearable. Then Jesus spoke again: "What do you want Me to do for you?" It couldn't be true. This was too much like a dream. Would he dare to open up his heart to Jesus?

What did Bartimaeus want of Jesus? Not money. Others could give him that. He needed much more than money. "Master," he said, "let me receive my sight." It was the prayer of every blind man, woman, and child since blindness first visited mankind. It is a prayer that always touches the soft heart of God and of His Son. But this particular prayer went deeper than the surface cry of despair and longing. Underneath it Jesus found something more. "And Jesus said to him, 'Go your way; your faith has made you well' " (Mark 10:52 RSV).

Bartimaeus had seen in Jesus more than the sighted multitudes around Him. John the Baptist had sent his own doubting disciples to Jesus to ask Him if He was the Messiah who was to come or if they should wait for another. Jesus sent back the message: "Go and tell John what you hear and see: the blind receive their sight and the lame walk ..." (Matt. 11:4–6). By this miracle the multitude with Jesus would be able to identify Him for what He was. Unfortunately they saw in Jesus, going to Jerusalem and His crucifixion, the son of David, royal descendant of their once great and glorious king, but not the Son of God, the Only-begotten of the Father, full of grace and truth. They saw in Jesus their potential emancipator from Roman military occupation, not the Redeemer who had come to destroy the works of the devil and to break the bondage of sin.

Bartimaeus found the mercy of the Savior, and it covered more than his sins. It removed for him the blindness of his eyes. He was one of those who were literally sitting in great darkness and saw a great Light.

The Penitent Malefactor

Lord, remember me when You come into Your kingdom.
Luke 23:42 NKJV

Just, Just in Time

DON'T be surprised to find faith just about any-where—except in hell. In a child, in a dying old man, in a king or a beggar, in a soldier or a merchant, in a tax collector or a prophet, in a fallen woman or a pious matron. Even in a criminal hanging on a cross, a few gasps from death.

Two thieves, traditionally named Dysmas and Testas, were crucified with Jesus on Good Friday. Dysmas had only to glance to his left to see the suffering Man nailed to the center cross. And looking above the Man's head, he could make out the accusation posted in mocking title: JESUS OF NAZARETH, KING OF THE JEWS.

Strange, no one was treating this Jesus like a king. Rather He was being mistreated as though He were the greatest criminal on Golgotha. From the moment He was cruelly nailed hand and foot to the accursed tree, the bystanders, from rulers and priests to soldiers and rabble, railed at Him. Even Testas was drawn into the ghastly game. Dysmas could understand that he and Testas deserved such treatment, but there was nothing in the center Man to merit such torture. Why, He wasn't even worthy of death!

Gradually Dysmas began to see in Jesus more than a bruised and bloodied remnant of a man. He heard Jesus praying for crucifiers! He saw Him bearing the cross and its shame without cursing. This kind of meekness and love stood out in that setting of violence and hatred. More than that, Jesus was mockingly being called the "Son of God." That was the answer! All of it made sense if Jesus was really the Son of God. The superscription on His cross was true: Jesus was the King, not only of the Jews but also of the everlasting kingdom of heaven. That crown of thorns made His crown of glory more splendid. Those scars in His hands and feet were proof that God is Love and that He has no pleasure in the death of the wicked, but that the wicked should turn from his way and live. And that blood trickling down that body and cross—the blood of God's Son—could cleanse him of all his sins. For that was the Lamb of God being sacrificed for Dysmas and the world before his very eyes!

Dysmas believed. And just in time. In a few hours the last chance to return to his heavenly Father would have vanished forever. There was no time left to make up for a lifetime squandered on himself. But all that he needed was on that center cross. How near and how adequately and how opportunely the love of God reaches out to the sinner! Glancing to the left, he could see the door to the Father's house ajar the width of a cross, just wide enough for him to squeeze through and into the light beyond.

"Jesus," cried Dysmas. The name of salvation was first announced in a night turned into day by the brightness of many joyous angels. Now it is spoken in a day turned into night by the sins of many creatures. Calling upon that name in faith saves. Dysmas called upon it and was told: "Truly, I say to you, today you will be with Me in Paradise" (Luke 23:43 RSV).

Dysmas saw in Jesus the only One who could save him even so late. And Jesus saw in Dysmas a brand to be snatched from the burning. He extended to the lifelong sinner the robe of sainthood washed white in His own blood.

The faith of Dysmas was not just adequate. It was extraordinary, considering the circumstances. He not only confessed his utter unworthiness, but he acknowledged Jesus to be the King of heaven. He counted on Jesus to perform everything necessary for his redemption. And he even tried to do a little mission work with his newfound faith. By publicly confessing his faith in Jesus and reproving the other criminal for his sins, he was witnessing to the Lord.

The malefactor's faith shines still brighter when we see it in its gloomy Good Friday setting. As yet there was no Easter on the calendar to confirm his faith. But for him the dying Lord on the center cross was victorious already, and Easter was certain to take place. He wanted an appointment in heaven with the Lord whom he expected to find there alive in glory.

Dysmas moved from the right hand of grace to the

right hand of glory in a few moments. For many a wrongdoer that journey covers many years, and some miss the glory because they scorn the grace. Dysmas arrived safe at his goal. He saw his last chance and caught his Savior's hand just in time.

Peter

Jesus immediately reached out His hand and caught him.

Matt. 14:31 RSV

The Fallen Can Stand Too

DOES the life of a drowning person flash before him as he sinks for the last time? Who knows? Yet the story of Peter's faith life is captured in that miraculous water-walking experience of his on the Sea of Galilee.

Peter and the other disciples were rowing hard against the wind late at night. Suddenly the Lord Jesus appeared to them, walking on the water. To make sure it was not a ghost, Peter challenged the figure: "Lord, if it is You, bid me come to You on the water." The answer was, "Come!" "So Peter got out of the boat *and walked on the water*" (Matt. 14:29). Look! He could do the seemingly impossible! He could imitate the Son of God!

The miracle did not last long, however. When Peter saw the wind lifting the waves around him, he faltered and sank. On his own, the weight of his human nature pulled him down. And "Jesus immediately reached out His hand and caught him, saying to him, 'O man of little faith, why did you doubt?' " (Matt. 14:31 RSV).

Later again it was nighttime, and Peter tried once

more to do what seems humanly impossible: he tried to remain loyal to the Lord while trusting in his own strength. He had felt pretty sure of himself. "Even if I must die with You, I will not deny You," he promised Jesus. But the waves of suspicion, ridicule, possible imprisonment, even martyrdom, rose to threaten him in the questions of the servants around the campfire. Peter, losing sight of his Lord and seeing just the waves, began to sink. Before the rooster crowed twice, Peter was going down for the third time,

He looked up then, and there was the Lord. All he could do was cry in his heart to the Savior: "Lord, save me!"

Then came Easter and the reinstatement on the shore of Galilee. Jesus was reaching out His hand again to poor Simon. He was still nearby, only a look and a call away. On the shores of that very sea Peter had heard His voice invite him: "Follow Me, and I will make you a fisher of men." Now He was saying: "Feed My lambs ... Feed My sheep." Again the impossible. Would Peter make it this time?

He didn't have to wait long to find out. One day the court that had condemned Jesus to the cross was asking Peter: "Do you know this Man?" Now Peter did not falter or hedge. The reply was strong and clear: "There is salvation in no one else, for there is no other name under heaven given among men by which we must be saved" (Acts 4:12 RSV). Back in the courtyard of Caiaphas, Peter had been terrified that the servants had seen him with Jesus. Now, in the court of Caiaphas, "when they saw the boldness of Peter ... they recognized that [he] had been with Jesus" (Acts 4:13 RSV). Now Peter corroborated the suspicion of his Lord's enemies with a fearless confession.

Now Simon was living up to the name Christ had given him, "Rock-man." He had discovered that to be solid he needed to stand upon the Rock of Ages, upon "that living Stone, rejected by men but in God's sight chosen and precious," a cornerstone laid by God (1 Peter 2:4–7 RSV).

Peter had learned that "it is better to trust in the Lord than to put confidence in man." Mindful of his failures because of self-confidence, he wrote in his First Epistle: " 'God opposes the proud, but gives grace to the humble.' Humble yourselves therefore under the mighty hand of God, that in due time He may exalt you' " (1 Peter 5:5–6 RSV).

This was something to remember when he stood before his own cross. Even there the Hand was outstretched to uphold him.

STEPHEN

And they stoned Stephen, calling upon God.

Acts 7:59

KILLED IN ACTION

SOME soldiers never get to see the Purple Heart they have won for heroism. They die as they earn the award. The medal is given to their families after their death.

In the long list of martyrs in the New Testament age, Stephen stands as the first Christian "killed in action." At the climax of his heroic defense of the faith, a volley of stones fell upon him as he knelt praying the prayer of his Lord: "Lord Jesus, receive my spirit." "Lord, do not hold this sin against them." Stephen did not live to see the far-reaching effect this loyalty to the end had upon the infant church.

Stephen was not a pastor. He was a layman in the Jerusalem congregation of the Christian church. In the course of time he had been appointed to the office of deacon. His duty was to see that the widows of the Greek Christians were not neglected. As he performed this office, Stephen was practicing the "pure and undefiled religion" described by St. James (1:27 NKJV). This meant visiting the widows and fatherless in their affliction and keeping himself unspotted from the world. This kind of religion is for every Christian to practice, pastor and layman alike. Stephen was a model of it. And he backed up his charity work with persuasive testimony so that those who disputed with him "could not withstand the wisdom and the Spirit with which he spoke" (Acts 6:10 RSV).

No one quarreled with Stephen's charity work. It was with the latter "plus" that he ran into trouble. Stephen's fault, as they saw it, was not that he had an inner conviction about Christ, but that he dared to be vocal about it. But Stephen felt that he had a confession to make, and he was going to make it. For it was this faith that had changed his life and made him truly concerned about the poor and neglected people. It was this faith that had brought him, orphaned and wretched in sin, into the bliss of the heavenly Father's family.

Though his critics kept on harassing Stephen, they failed to silence him. They would have to resort to more forceful means. So a group of them secretly instigated some false witnesses to bring a charge of blasphemy against Stephen before the council. Now this was the same accusation that was laid to Jesus before the very same Sanhedrin. At that time too the high priest expressed amazed indignation at the accused standing before him. All around him Stephen could see men who, as Jesus had said, "devour widows' houses, and for a pretense make long prayers" (Matt. 23:14). Stephen stood before them, his face like that of an angel. The council ranged about him, gnashing their teeth at him in rage. The contrast continues to the very end. Stephen stood gazing into heaven, his eyes glistening with the vision of the Son of God standing at the right hand of God. They cried with a loud voice as they stopped their ears and rushed together upon him, cast him out of the city, and stoned him.

There Stephen fell to his knees, praying the prayer of forgiveness his Lord had prayed for these same people. "And when he had said this, he fell asleep" (Acts 7:60).

If medals were given for this type of bravery and loyalty, they would have to be awarded to Stephen's heirs (in this case, the church, us) posthumously, and they might very well be inscribed with the words of Heb. 11:38: "Of whom the world was not worthy."

PAUL

I know whom I have believed.

2 Tim. 1:12

"I Know!"

YOU see something happen. It happens to you. It seems unbelievable. Someone asks you to prove what you are reporting. What do you do? Whatever you do, you say, "It is so! I know!" Eventually the argument has to stop. There is no rebuttal to "I know!" except the cruel accusation "You must be out of your mind. It cannot be!"

Paul heard this kind of remark and insinuation many times after he saw the Lord Jesus on the road to Damascus. Especially when he placed the miracle of Jesus' resurrection before people. And yet, what else could he do? He had seen the risen Jesus with his eyes. And the sight had turned him around in his tracks.

Before the vision, Paul was Saul, a self-righteous, zealous persecutor of the Way and of those who walked the Way. Then Saul felt no need for a Savior. Jesus was superfluous. In fact, Jesus was a threat to the monument Saul was building of his own life, inscribed SAUL. Jesus was someone to kick out of the way, even if you hurt your toes doing so. He was competition for the current ruler of Saul's heart and life, that is, Saul.

Now all this has changed. And the point of change had been that vision of the risen crucified Lord Jesus saying: "Saul, be My special messenger." Eventually, that is what Saul became. With the change of his outlook and goal came a new name, Paul. And Paul was a new man, radically, different from the old. Paul saw the miracle of a new birth take place within himself. And he knew *who* caused it, not *what* caused it. It wasn't a question of reform, for the former Pharisee felt no need for reform. He thought he was perfectly acceptable to God as he was. It was simply this: Paul had been turned to God by having his feet set upon Him who is the only Way to the Father.

To Paul it was simple, a miracle, and a fact. But to those to whom he testified, the miracle was madness.

Faith cannot be scientifically investigated or described. It amounts to trusting in the unlikely, the unseen, the impossible. When Paul talked about Jesus, he was publicizing someone who could not be seen, whose body was not even around to check. When Paul explained that Jesus was God's Son, this was brushed off as unlikely. Of course, they would go along with the idea of a Supreme Being, but that this Supreme Being should have a Son who enclosed Himself in a human body, this was not only unlikely, it was preposterous. And to become even more fantastic: that this Man, crucified according to ancient prediction, died, was buried, and rose from the dead! This could be accepted only by faith.

All Paul could say was, "I know!" There were no doubts in his mind about it. He needed no scientific proof, he did not have to put his hands and fingers into the side and hands of Christ's body. He knew!

And because he knew what Christ was and what He had done, Paul knew what was waiting for him beyond the grave. "I know whom I have believed, and I am sure that He is able to guard until that Day what I have entrusted to Him" (2 Tim. 1:12 RSV). That's faith, when you can say, "I know!"

Such believers know the blessedness Jesus means when He says: "Blessed are they that have not seen, and yet have believed" (John 20:29).

AQUILA AND PRISCILLA

Greet Priscilla and Aquila, my fellow workers in Christ Jesus, who risked their necks for my life. ... Greet also the church in their house.

Rom. 16:3–5 RSV

NO LONGER TWO BUT ONE

JESUS came to reverse the results of Eden. Aquila and Priscilla, contemporaries of St. Paul and pioneers in the early church, are striking examples of His handiwork.

Paul first came across this wonderful couple in Corinth. They had recently fled there from Italy, "because Claudius had commanded all the Jews to leave Rome" (Acts 18:2 RSV). Aquila was a Jew, but his Roman wife Priscilla followed him into exile. After all, God had joined them together in marriage, and they weren't going to let even the emperor put them asunder. They were no longer two but one. For better or for worse they belonged together.

They were one in more than marriage. They were both converts to Christianity. And in Christ they were bound even more closely than just husband and wife. In

Christ, they discovered, "there is neither Jew nor Greek [nor Roman], there is neither slave nor free, there is neither male nor female; for you are all one in Christ Jesus" (Gal. 3:28 RSV). They were as one as Adam and Eve before the Fall, while both still shared the closest bond with the heavenly Father. What Adam and Eve forfeited by sin, Aquila and Priscilla found in Christ. Even the hazardous difference in national backgrounds was surmounted by their unity in the Lord.

When Adam and Eve disobeyed the will of God, their communication with God was disrupted. And out of their corruption came the first murderer. Aquila and Priscilla, having been born again into God's family by Baptism, comprised a little church in their own household. "For where two or three are gathered together in My name, there am I in the midst of them" (Matt. 18:20). Theirs was no divided marriage, one worshiping in his corner and the other in hers. Here were two people living under one roof as "heirs together of the grace of life," their prayers unhindered. (1 Peter 3:7)

Paul found something else in common with Aquila and Priscilla. They shared the same occupation. They were tentmakers. This was their means of earning a living to support their calling in Christ as witnesses to the love of God. They were tentmakers, or "tenters," as the Bible calls human beings on their earthly pilgrimage. At the same time with the Gospel they were offering to people eternal habitations not made with hands.

Adam and Eve, offering each other the forbidden fruit, were cast out of the home God had made for them. Aquila and Priscilla, offering the Bread of Life, were showing outcasts and prodigals the way back into the household of God.

Though Aquila and Priscilla were probably child-less, they became the godparents of numerous children of God. Apollo, a Jewish convert to Christ, was instruct-ed by Aquila and Priscilla, and many others owed their place in God's family to the seed planted by this devot-ed couple. The children of Adam and Eve inherited death from their parents; Aquila and Priscilla's "chil-dren" inherited life.

Paul owed Aquila and Priscilla a lifelong debt of gratitude. This dear couple had risked their necks to pro-tect the apostle in those dangerous days. As Adam and Eve were willing to risk death so that they might go their own way, Aquila and Priscilla ventured death so that some of God's precious creatures might go His way.

We could go on to admire this husband-and-wife team, pushing frontiers of the Kingdom outward, offer-ing their home to fugitives, transforming whoever passed through their hands and sending them out into the world amplified, edified, and sanctified.

But we might envy them most for having found and shown what it is to be "no longer two but one" in Christ Jesus.

TIMOTHY

A disciple was there, named Timothy, the son of a Jewish woman who was a believer; but his father was a Greek.

Acts 16:1 RSV

BEATING THE HANDICAP OF BIRTH

YOUNG Timothy gave no indication of being the mixed-up child of a mixed marriage.

He might have been. His believing mother and pagan father might have agreed at his birth that the child should be let alone in respect to his religious upbringing. They might have said: "Wait until he is older; then let him decide for himself what he wants to believe. As for now, we won't mention the subject."

And the child, seeing one parent interested in religion and the other lukewarm or indifferent, might have become confused as to what to believe or whether to believe in anything at all.

By the grace of God, Timothy escaped this spiritual disaster. Normally, in an all-Jewish household it was the responsibility of the father to bring up his children in the nurture and admonition of the Lord. God had prescribed for Israel that in this way His commandments, precepts, and promises should be transmitted from generation to generation. When Timothy's pagan father defaulted in this task, Eunice, his mother, and Lois, his grandmother, took over the basic religious training of the child.

As early as possible they set his little feet on the paths of righteousness and placed into his tiny hands the lamp to light his path. Paul reminded Timothy of this maternal influence in his life when he wrote to his pupil: "From childhood you have known the Holy Scriptures, which are able to make you wise for salvation" (2 Tim. 3:15 NKJV). Instead of the ephemeral wisdom of the Greek philosophers, Timothy was imbued with the wisdom exalted by Solomon and embodied in Jesus Christ. "And Greeks seek after wisdom; but we preach Christ crucified, to the Jews a stumbling block and to the Greeks foolishness, but to those who are called, both Jews and Greeks, Christ the power of God and the wisdom of God" (1 Cor. 1:22–24 NKJV). In the Scriptures, Timothy had found the wise will and plan of God for him and for all people in Christ.

Since Timothy had no spiritual father in his own home, St. Paul became Timothy's "father," begetting him as a child of God by the seed of the Gospel. The elder statesman of Christ liked to think of Timothy as his "own son in the faith," his "dearly beloved son." Now Timothy belonged. Now he was adopted into the very family of God. Now he could grow and flourish normally without the handicap of fractured emotions. His life was anchored and secure.

When his other assistants proved unreliable, Paul could turn confidently to Timothy to carry on the work he had begun. Writing to the Philippian Christians from his imprisonment, Paul gave Timothy this lofty endorsement: "I hope in the Lord Jesus to send Timothy to you soon, so that I may be cheered by news of you. I have no one like him, who will be genuinely anxious for your welfare. They all look after their own interests, not those of Jesus Christ. But Timothy's worth you know, how as a son with a father he has served with me in the gospel." (Phil. 2:19–22 RSV).

Timothy kept growing stronger and stronger in this loyalty to the cause of Christ. According to tradition, Timothy, as an elderly bishop in Ephesus, was confronted one last time with the power and pressure of Greek paganism. According to tradition he was killed while attempting to stop an indecent heathen procession during the festival of Diana.

From beginning to end he was all Christ's.

DORCAS (TABITHA)

She was full of good works and acts of charity.

Acts 9:36 RSV

"NOW THERE ABIDETH ... CHARITY"

THE evil that men do lives after them, the good is oft interred with their bones," was the cynical remark of grief-stricken Mark Antony at the death of Julius Caesar, according to Shakespeare. It isn't necessarily so. There is the case of Dorcas (or Tabitha), a certain follower of Jesus who lived in Joppa in the days of the apostles.

Good as she was, Dorcas had died, as everyone must. Considerately, her friends took care of the funeral arrangements. They laid out her corpse in an upper chamber until the hour of burial.

As the news of her death spread through the community, many gathered to pay their respects to the woman eulogized by the Bible as "full of good works and acts of charity." When it was learned that Peter was at nearby Lydda, he was called and arrived at the house, where "all the widows stood beside him weeping, and showing tunics and other garments which Dorcas made while she was with them" (Acts 9:39

RSV). Her friends were poorer by one good person, and a large quantity was subtracted from the supply of love in the world. The death of Dorcas was a great loss to those who were left behind.

Dorcas died, but the good that she had done went on living after her. It was like seed planted to bear fruit later. Like the coats and garments she had made for the poor, the coverings of love she had woven during her lifetime were still warming the chilled and lonely souls of many. She had been a fountain of kindness. Yet more amazing than the sudden shutting off of that fountain was the emergence of that fountain in the first place.

Dorcas was not just a certain woman living in Joppa, who happened to be a very charitable person. She is recorded for all time as a certain *disciple*. That meant that she was a follower, or pupil, of the Lord Jesus. This was the well of living water which had sprung up in her and which flowed forth to enrich the lives of others.

Love is something that comes from God, who is Love. No one produces it by himself. "If we love one another, God abides in us, and His love is perfected in us" (I John 4:12). "We know that we have passed from death to life, because we love the brethren. He who does not love his brother abides in death" (1 John 3:14 NKJV). God permitted Dorcas to be raised from the dead by Peter, in order for her to go on loving for a while longer, not in order to pass into life. She had already passed from death to life when she was raised from selfishness to service by her faith in Jesus Christ. She was alive for God because she followed Jesus. That was why she loved her neighbors.

She was raised from the death of the body in that upper chamber. It was in an upper room that Jesus showed His disciples how they could demonstrate the risen life He had come to give them. There He took a towel and girded Himself and washed the feet of His disciples and said to them: "Do you know what I have done to you? You call Me Teacher and Lord; and you are right, for so I am. If I then, your Lord and Teacher, have washed your feet, you also ought to wash one another's feet. For I have given you an example, that you also should do as I have done to you" (John 13:12–15 RSV).

Dorcas had learned the meaning of discipleship. It consists in following; following Jesus obediently, following Him in trust, following Him in love and in sacrifice, following Him through death into life eternal with the Father. Dorcas was that kind of disciple. There were the coats and garments to prove it.

LYDIA

If you have judged me to be faithful to the Lord, come to my house and stay.

Acts 16:15 RSV

THE BEST PURPLE ANYWHERE

THE world of business can be a dangerous arena. It is filled with victims who have been scarred in cutthroat combat with ruthless competitors. Certain ventures on that battlefield end in ulcers, dishonesty, scandal, or even death. The stakes are high, the ground rules are tough, and the casualties are legion.

In that agitated arena stood a certain woman named Lydia, a native of Thyatira. She was a seller of purple, an expensive textile, in the city of Philippi. All indications hint that she was a successful career woman.

Her brief biography in Acts 16 states that she was also a worshiper of God. Today that would be nothing unusual. Many business people are members of the church. But then, in Philippi, it was worth remarking that Lydia was both a businesswoman and a worshiper of the true God. As difficult as it is to be both today, a merchant and a consistent believer, it was more difficult then.

The entire city was pagan. People who did not worship the gods of the Greeks stood out among the majority. And merchants who were not pagans were even more conspicuous. In fact, they were asking for a hard struggle. The heathen merchants were wary of competition as it was, but they were particularly on guard against nonpagan competition. It was in that very city that Paul and Silas were framed and jailed by the owners of a slave girl who became a Christian because of their preaching and who stopped making money for her owners by fortunetelling. Lydia dared to be a merchant and a worshiper of God under those circumstances.

Running into such obstacles, Lydia might have felt that she had done enough to have made a gesture in the direction of religious affiliation. She might have felt it wise to play down her church connections and gradually to push her faith into the background. She could turn to it if she had to. Or she might exploit her religious ties to get a few Jewish and Christian customers. But she did none of these things.

Rather she made her position more hazardous by opening her heart to the Gospel and being baptized a Christian. The circle in which she was enclosed now grew smaller still. There were at least more Jews in the city than Christians, and if the Jews had only the pagans against them, as a Christian she would have both the pagans and the Jews boycotting her store. But this did not stop Lydia either. She proceeded to have her entire household baptized, and then she opened her home to the apostles as a church.

There is no record of her having abandoned her career at this point. Instead she converted it too into a calling and used it to serve the Lord and her fellowmen.

She, who knew the value of purple goods, discovered the priceless value of the garment of righteousness woven of crimson strands on the loom of the cross. She knew that the wearer of that "purple" would be marked as a royal priest before God. Not only she herself could now wear this garment, but her customers and friends, admiring it, would desire to have one like it themselves. And she could tell them where to get it, not wholesale, but completely free of charge.

Prior to her conversion, Lydia could offer the Philippians the finest quality of goods, patrician purple. Now those who came to her store could find there the best "purple" anywhere.